I Just Got Saved!

What Have I Done?

KEITH BRUMBALOW

I Just Got Saved! What Have I Done?

Copyright © 2023 Keith Brumbalow

Paperback Book ISBN-13: 979-8-9896506-1-3

EBook ISBN-13: 979-8-9896506-0-6

Cover design by: Keith Brumbalow

Visit us at Kbrumwrites.com

DEDICATION

To my Lord and Savior, Jesus Christ, for His saving grace and unwavering love.

To Carol, my wife of over 45 years, our three children, Steven, Kelly, and Kari, daughter-in-law Amanda, and grandson Elijah.

CONTENTS

INTRODUCTION

You were in a church service, talking with a friend at school, discussing religion with your parents or sibling, or having lunch with a coworker, when suddenly you realized what they were telling you was true. You were on your way to an eternity in hell, and you needed to do something about it. Your decision was to acknowledge your sinful condition and your need for a Savior and ask Christ to forgive you, which He did.

Perhaps a short while later, you are asking yourself, "What have I done?"

My hope is that this book will provide an answer to this and other questions you may have about your personal decision to ask Christ to save you. Becoming a Christian happens instantly, the moment you give your heart to Jesus, but understanding the Christian life will take the remaining time you have on earth, as it is vast, and we will always be learning. Do not let this discourage you; rather, let it help you understand how relevant and timeless God's Word is. No one will ever fully know the depth of the scriptures until we are home in heaven.

Note that there are plenty of books available to discuss each of the topics in this book in much more depth. My aim was to present these topics to the new believer as a help toward familiarizing them with their new-found faith.

If you are reading this book, and you have never trusted Christ as your Savior, perhaps you will find answers to questions you have, answers that may lead you closer to making your own salvation decision—before it is too late.

Throughout this book, we will be using scripture references from the Authorized King James Bible, the only Bible I would recommend for final biblical authority. I trust you will investigate these references by reading them on your own, in your own Bible, and their surrounding scriptures for proper context. Let God's Word become a regular part of your everyday life.

I JUST GOT SAVED! WHAT HAVE I DONE?

Wow! Congratulations! Whether you realize it now or not, accepting Jesus Christ as your personal Savior is the most important decision you have made, or will ever make. It far outweighs your choice of college, place of employment, selection of a spouse, names for your children, where you want to live, or any other direction of opportunity you may take. All these other things may change in your life, but your salvation will never change, because the One Who saved us never changes.

Hebrews 13:8 Jesus Christ the same yesterday, and today, and forever.

Becoming a Christian changed your life forever. No, the earth did not shake, the sky did not split open, there was no sudden appearance of a heavenly angelic host shouting, "Hallelujah!" but a change did take place. You may or may not have cried for joy or been overcome with emotions immediately following your conversion. You may not have felt anything at all. Please understand that

7

salvation is not a feeling, it is a transformation. You have been transformed from a soul that had no hope and was destined for hell, to a soul full of hope and destined for heaven; something definitely worth being joyful over.

Your sins have been forgiven!

Colossians 1:14 In whom we have redemption through his blood, even the forgiveness of sins:

Acts 10:43 To him give all the prophets witness, that through his name whosoever believeth in him shall receive remission of sins.

Hebrews 8:12 For I will be merciful to their unrighteousness, and their sins and their iniquities will I remember no more.

Jesus died for the sins of the entire world, but that only made salvation possible for everyone, not automatic. Receiving Christ is a personal decision that we each must make on our own, and when we do, He forgives us of our sin debt. This does not mean we will never sin again. We were not made perfect when we got saved, just forgiven. You will sin again, probably every day, but it should not be your habit to continue in sin. Nor should you use the fact that God will forgive you as an excuse to sin. We should strive to live a holy life pleasing to God. And when we do sin, we can confess these sins to God, and he will forgive us if we repent from them.

1John 1:9 If we confess our sins, he is faithful and just to forgive us our sins, and to cleanse us from all unrighteousness.

Confessing our sins should be a daily prayer to God that we might keep ourselves clean for His service.

The day you invited Christ into your life, you became a new creation. Unlike an old antique car, God did not disassemble and rebuild you, or physically remake you in any way. In fact, no one will be able to tell from your physical appearance that anything has changed at all. You are still the same person you were before, except now you have a new perspective.

2Corinthians 5:17 Therefore if any man be in Christ, he is a new creature: old things are passed away; behold, all things are become new.

You now view things in light of your own salvation. Your attitude and desires will change, and you will want to tell others what has happened to you.

A void has been filled by God that satisfies your soul unlike anything else you may have tried—good or bad. You may have tried things that took exorbitant amounts of your time and talent to mask the emptiness you felt inside. Turning over a new leaf did not work. New Year's resolutions did not work. Doing good deeds did not work. All these humanistic, life-changing attempts left emptiness within, and you knew you were still missing something. Every human soul has a hollow spot that can be filled only by God, and nothing else will do. A person will search life's depths, follow friends' advice, try all kinds of mechanical changes in their life, all out of desperation to fill that void. Though you still have the same hair color, height, voice, and shoe size, God has made changes in your life; not on the outside, but on the inside. And it was the result of nothing you could have done for yourself.

When you asked Jesus to save you and come into your life, He took your invitation seriously, so, God sent His Holy Spirit to live within you. Imagine that! God's spirit lives within you! Perhaps you have heard the phrase, 'Your body is a temple.' Now that you are a Christian, your body houses God's spirit and, thus, is His temple.

1Corinthians 6:19–20 What? know ye not that your body is the temple of the Holy Ghost which is in you, which ye have of God, and ye are not your own? For ye are bought with a price: therefore glorify God in your body, and in your spirit, which are God's.

Jesus paid the price for our sin when He gave Himself as the sinless sacrifice on the cross of Calvary. He offered Himself willingly to pay a debt we could not pay. And not for you or me only, but for the whole world. If you have accepted Him as your Savior, you belong to God.

You have been reborn! Not in a physical sense, but your spirit has been reborn to new life.

1Peter 1:23 Being born again, not of corruptible seed, but of incorruptible, by the word of God, which liveth and abideth forever.

Before you got saved, your spirit was as good as dead since you were on your way to hell. Nothing on earth could have helped you or changed your spiritual condition or eternal destination.

John 3:18 He that believeth on him is not condemned: but he that believeth not is condemned already, because he hath not believed in the name of the only begotten Son of God.

When you called upon Jesus to save you and received God's spirit, you were regenerated unto life eternal, and your spirit was made alive unto God. Now, there is nothing on earth or anywhere else that can change the fact that you are on your way to heaven.

Spiritually speaking, when you first get saved, you are a babe in Christ, and all things in the spiritual realm appear new to you (e.g., the Bible, church, Christian behavior, relationship with Christ, Bible doctrine, etc.). And, depending on your upbringing and familiarity with church life, some things may even appear a little strange like objects outside the womb appear to a newborn infant. But, just as all infants grow physically in time from proper nourishment and become familiar with their surroundings, you will continue to mature in your spirituality as you grow in the Lord by reading your Bible, praying to God, attending church, and fellowshipping with other believers.

1Peter 2:2 As newborn babes, desire the sincere milk of the word, that ye may grow thereby:

In this verse, Peter encourages new believers to study the Word of God (the Bible) to build a scriptural foundation of fundamental truths. After this foundation is laid, the believer can continue his Bible study to build his knowledge and understanding of biblical principles and doctrine.

You are now one of the fold. In the New Testament, Christians are often metaphorically referred to as sheep and Jesus as our Good Shepherd. Just as sheep learn to recognize and follow the voice of their shepherd, we continually learn more about our Savior and desire to follow His teachings as we read His Word. The Holy Spirit speaks to our heart as we read and teaches us personal applications of scripture. If we are obedient to our Shepherd, as most sheep are to their human shepherd, then we will listen to His teachings and follow Christ as the Holy Spirit leads us. Jesus said;

John 10:27–28 My sheep hear my voice, and I know them, and they follow me: And I give unto them eternal life; and they shall never perish, neither shall any man pluck them out of my hand.

You are in the hand of Christ! There is no safer place for sheep than with their shepherd, and there is no greater Shepherd than Jesus.

You have been adopted into the family of God as one of His children! Though Jesus is the only begotten Son of God, you have been grafted in by God's grace and mercy and now have the privilege to call God, Father.

Romans 8:15–17 For ye have not received the spirit of bondage again to fear; but ye have received the Spirit of adoption, whereby we cry, Abba, Father. The Spirit itself beareth witness with our spirit, that we are the children of God: And if children, then heirs; heirs of God, and joint-heirs with Christ; if so be that we suffer with him, that we may be also glorified together.

Just like a child when he has been physically adopted into a new family is given full liberty and access to his new parents, you now have full liberty and access to God's throne. You can approach Him anytime in prayer and talk with Him as a friend. God will grant you access to anything that will help conform you more into the image of His Son, Jesus Christ, and to fulfill His will for your life.

Your heavenly Father desires to see you grow in faith and mature as a Christian.

Galations 3:26 For ye are all the children of God by faith in Christ Jesus.

You have found a faithful friend in Jesus. Perhaps you have, or have had, some very close friends in your life that you would trust with anything. Can you tell them your innermost secrets or share your real hurts and fears with total confidence they will earnestly listen and offer honest feedback? Will they truly understand your feelings and offer the unconditional support you need in a loving, yet forthright manner? Jesus is such a friend and more! While on earth, Jesus experienced every human emotion and was tempted beyond measure yet overcame it all—without sin. Today, He is seated at the right hand of God's throne listening to our prayers and offering the compassion, wisdom, and guidance we need to help us live a fruitful Christian life that is pleasing to Him. He is the answer to all our troubles and heartaches and the supplier of all our needs.

Jesus is a friend that will never leave us nor forsake us.

Hebrews 13:5 Let your conversation be without covetousness; and be content with such things as ye have: for he hath said, I will never leave thee, nor forsake thee.

Friends will come and go, even good friends. Some will be your close friend on Monday, not so close on Tuesday, and then close again on Wednesday. Jesus is always your best friend with no variation in character.

James 1:17 Every good gift and every perfect gift is from above, and cometh down from the Father of lights, with whom is no variableness, neither shadow of turning.

Malachi 3:6 For I am the LORD, I change not;

Jesus will never turn His back and walk away from us no matter what we do. He does not condone our sin but wants to help us get victory over our sin. His attitude and love toward us will never change. He loved us before we ever got saved.

Romans 5:8 But God commendeth his love toward us, in that, while we were yet sinners, Christ died for us.

Jesus performed the ultimate display of friendship when He died for us on the cross.

John 15:13 Greater love hath no man than this, that a man lay down his life for his friends.

We are truly most blessed to have a friend like Jesus.

You now have a personal Comforter. The disciples who physically walked with Jesus received personal instructions from Jesus concerning Himself, God, and salvation's plan for the world. At times they sat for hours listening to His teachings, captivated by His wisdom as he spoke with supreme authority. As long as He was with them, they felt bold and were comforted in knowing He would take care of them, as demonstrated in the miracles they witnessed Him perform. Several times during His three-and-one-half-year earthly ministry Jesus told the disciples that the time would come when He would be taken from them to be crucified for the sins of the world. The disciples found this hard to believe, not yet understanding the necessity of His death on the cross, and were bewildered to a degree. To calm their fears, He told them that, though He would be gone, His Father would not leave them comfortless but would send His Spirit to reside in the hearts of believers.

John 14:16–17 And I will pray the Father, and he shall give you another Comforter, that he may abide with you forever; Even the Spirit of truth; whom the world cannot receive, because it seeth him not, neither knoweth him: but ye know him; for he dwelleth with you, and shall be in you.

Today, the Comforter—the Holy Spirit—gives us comfort when we need it, and boldness to proclaim the Word of God to others, just as He did for the early disciples.

The Holy Spirit is also our teacher.

John 14:26 But the Comforter, which is the Holy Ghost, whom the Father will send in my name, he shall teach you all things, and bring all things to your remembrance, whatsoever I have said unto you.

The Holy Spirit speaks to our heart as we read God's Word to help us understand the text and how we might personally apply it to our life. He helps us understand the Bible in a way that unbelievers cannot.

1Corinthians 2:14 But the natural man receiveth not the things of the Spirit of God: for they are foolishness unto him: neither can he know them, because they are spiritually discerned.

Many may say that they have tried to read the Bible, but they cannot understand it. There may be a good reason for that; they may not be saved.

The Holy Spirit will also "bring all things to your remembrance" as it applies to scripture. You may find yourself in a conversation with someone when suddenly a scripture verse that you've studied before comes to mind that is needed in your situation. This recall is from the Holy Spirit helping you to be a witness for Christ.

WHAT AM I SAVED FROM?

By now, you must know that you have been saved from utter destruction and eternal torment in hell.

Mark 16:16 He that believeth and is baptized shall be saved; but he that believeth not shall be damned.

We may be familiar to some degree with what torment is, but it is hard for us to fathom eternity since it has no dimensions. We cannot quantify it by tagging a time limit to it or compare it to any time measure we are familiar with, as time simply does not apply. It is like trying to give a definitive answer to the quotient of one divided by zero. Pick any other number besides zero and you can always get a real answer, no matter how large or small, but zero can only yield infinity, which is incomprehensible. Eternity simply has no end, which may be why some will ignore its finality and pretend it does not exist; death will make them oh so aware.

Christians will never know the full depth of hell. Jesus told us it is an awful place.

Mark 9:44 Where their worm dieth not, and the fire is not quenched.

He gave us a real-life example of a man who died and opened his eyes in hell.

Luk 16:23–24 And in hell he lifted up his eyes, being in torments, and seeth Abraham afar off, and Lazarus in his bosom. And he cried and said, Father Abraham, have mercy on me, and send Lazarus, that he may dip the tip of his finger in water, and cool my tongue; for I am tormented in this flame.

He begged for just a drop of water to touch his tongue, but no water would be given. It is interesting, yet sad to note, that Jesus told this story almost 2000 years ago and that man is still in hell today, yet to receive any relief from his pain or suffering.

We can imagine hell as a deep dark abyss that possesses the souls of unbelievers (the unsaved) and offers no compassion, encouragement, comfort, pleasure, counseling, fellowship, companionship, rest, or contentment for them. Anyone who ever says he is going to party in hell simply has no idea what he is talking about. It is said that misery loves company, but no one in hell is comforted. Instead, the unbelievers will forever be tormented physically by the flames and pain, and mentally by remembering every chance they ever had to accept Jesus as their personal Savior, and nothing will ever be done to change their situation. Mindful of their eternal and inescapable punishment, we do not brag about our salvation, but we offer continual praise to God as we think of what He has done for us, and how we could be one of those lost souls.

We have been saved from our old life and old ways, and as stated earlier, each of us has become a new creature.

2Corinthians 5:17 Therefore if any man be in Christ, he is a new creature: old things are passed away; behold, all things are become new.

For those who have been saved for a while, we can look back on our old self and see that things are definitely different. Our habits have changed to now include spiritual things. There are some things we no longer do, which have been exchanged for better deeds. The Bible instructs us to put away our old, sinful deeds and seek to become more like Christ.

Colossians 3:8–10 But now ye also put off all these; anger, wrath, malice, blasphemy, filthy communication out of your mouth. Lie not one to another, seeing that ye have put off the old man with his deeds; And have put on the new man, which is renewed in knowledge after the image of him that created him:

Ephesians 4:22–24 That ye put off concerning the former conversation the old man, which is corrupt according to the deceitful lusts; And be renewed in the spirit of your mind; And that ye put on the new man, which after God is created in righteousness and true holiness.

Our old life offered neither hope nor positive direction for our future, as there is no hope without God.

19

Ephesians 2:12–13 That at that time ye were without Christ, being aliens from the commonwealth of Israel, and strangers from the covenants of promise, having no hope, and without God in the world: But now in Christ Jesus ye who sometimes were far off are made nigh by the blood of Christ.

1Timothy 1:1 Paul, an apostle of Jesus Christ by the commandment of God our Savior, and Lord Jesus Christ, which is our hope;

We may have thought we knew where we were headed in life and what we wanted before we got saved, but nothing satisfied until we invited Christ into our life. No longer do we live without purpose, as we now carry the love of God to share it with others in hope that they might trust Him as their Savior, too. Our mission is now clear and has not changed since Jesus issued the orders.

Matthew 28:19–20 Go ye therefore, and teach all nations, baptizing them in the name of the Father, and of the Son, and of the Holy Ghost: Teaching them to observe all things whatsoever I have commanded you: and, lo, I am with you always, even unto the end of the world.

You are saved from the power of sin. That is not to say you will never sin again, but, if you do, it is your choice. Before you were saved, sin had its control over you because you had no inner strength with which to resist, and your old man was alive to sin. Your old man has been crucified with Christ on the cross of Calvary and your new man should no longer be drawn to sin. Now, the Holy Spirit abides within you, and He will give you strength to resist and convict you when you cross the line.

Romans 6:6–14 Knowing this, that our old man is crucified with him, that the body of sin might be destroyed, that henceforth we should not serve sin. For he that is dead is freed from sin. Now if we be dead with Christ, we believe that we shall also live with him: Knowing that Christ being raised from the dead dieth no more; death hath no more dominion over him. For in that he died, he died unto sin once: but in that he liveth, he liveth unto God. Likewise reckon ye also yourselves to be dead indeed unto sin, but alive unto God through Jesus Christ our Lord. Let not sin therefore reign in your mortal body, that ye should obey it in the lusts thereof. Neither yield ye your members as instruments of unrighteousness unto sin: but yield yourselves unto God, as those that are alive from the dead, and your members as instruments of righteousness unto God. For sin shall not have dominion over you: for ye are not under the law, but under grace.

HOW LONG DOES SALVATION LAST?

Let us establish our part in the transformation of our soul, called salvation. Receiving salvation cannot be compared with membership of a club, group, or association. There are no membership fees, no required academic or social achievements, or any expiration of acceptance. There are no coupons to give you a special deal and no levels of clearance that limit your access. The only criteria are that you have repented from your sins, confessed unto God what you believe about Christ, and called upon Him to save you. Your act of faith to trust that Jesus will save you, just as He said He would, invites the Holy Spirit into your heart. And you did absolutely nothing to earn it!

We are totally incapable of doing anything to merit God's gift of salvation on our own, so, if we cannot save ourselves from the condemnation of hell, then how can we keep ourselves saved? We must rely on the sustaining power of the Holy Spirit.

Ephesians 1:13 In whom ye also trusted, after that ye heard the word of truth, the gospel of your salvation: in whom also after that ye believed, ye were sealed with that holy Spirit of promise,

Ephesians 4:30 And grieve not the Holy Spirit of God, whereby ye are sealed unto the day of redemption.

It is He, the Holy Spirit, that watches over our soul and keeps us in the fold of the kingdom of God. It is He that fights our spiritual battles for us and gives us victory. Satan can claim no hold on us because he knows we possess the Spirit of God.

Salvation was made possible by the blood sacrifice of Jesus Christ on the cross of Calvary. Though in the Old Testament, the High Priest offered a blood sacrifice for the people of Israel, it was a limited atonement, or payment, and had to be repeated every year. The animals used in the sacrifices were the best the people had to offer but were still only a poor picture of the ultimate sacrifice that would come later in Jesus. The atonement of Jesus is sufficient in that He offered Himself only once for the sins of the entire world, past, present, and future.

Hebrews 10:12 But this man, after he had offered one sacrifice for sins forever, sat down on the right hand of God;

So, we cannot do anything to earn salvation, and we have no power to hang on to salvation. We simply play no part in our salvation other than calling on Jesus to save us. Jesus finished the work of salvation on the cross of Calvary and the Holy Spirit preserves our salvation. It is God's gift to us. Once we accept it, we cannot lose it.

WHAT DO I DO NOW?

If you have not already, thank God for what He has done for you. Living your life without God was a spiritual struggle over your soul, whether you have recognized it or not. Maybe you had felt the unrelenting pressures and guilt that haunted your mind as you battled over the years questioning your eternal destination. Maybe some days you felt your prospects of going to heaven were pretty good, at least as good as some of the so-called Christians you knew, while other days you knew without a doubt you were on your way to hell. That struggle is finally over! Your eternity is forever settled! You have won the ultimate victory, but there will be other battles along the way. Becoming a Christian did not make you physically indestructible, nor did it line your pockets with gold or take away all your worries and cares. Jesus told us we would still have problems, but He is there to help us, and He can overcome anything.

> *John 16:33 These things I have spoken unto you, that in me ye might have peace. In the world ye shall have tribulation: but be of good cheer; I have overcome the world.*

Your mission now is to become trained and equipped to take the gospel message to others.

Marathon athletes give it their all as they fight to win one of the most grueling foot races established for measuring a runner's endurance. Most have trained for years for this relatively short period of time and are prepared to totally empty themselves of energy to achieve their goal. Once they have crossed the finish line, many will collapse from exhaustion, and all will feel a sense of relief that the race is over. Though the professional athlete will be disappointed to not win, the satisfaction the amateur feels to have just finished will be quite evident on their face. When your spiritual struggle is over, you can express the same depth of relief when you get saved, but it is not time for you to rest in your decision of having accepted Christ as your Savior and be satisfied with looking back. On the contrary, your race in the Christian life has just begun. The finish line the Christian is looking for is at death, when our life on earth is done. Until that day comes, we race.

Like any foot race, there can only be one winner crowned at the finish line, who is often celebrated as a star and is lavished with gifts and honor. In time, the gifts vanish, the honor wanes, and the athlete is all but forgotten. In the Bible, the Apostle Paul explained that this is not the kind of race the Christian runs.

1Corinthians 9:24–27 Know ye not that they which run in a race run all, but one receiveth the prize? So run, that ye may obtain. And every man that striveth for the mastery is temperate in all things. Now they do it to obtain a corruptible crown; but we an incorruptible. I therefore so run, not as uncertainly; so fight I, not as one that

26

beateth the air: But I keep under my body, and bring it into subjection: lest that by any means, when I have preached to others, I myself should be a castaway.

When our race on this earth is finally over, we will receive rewards for every good deed we have done in our Christian walk. These rewards will not rust or fade away but will be incorruptible. These are the kinds of treasures Jesus told us we should strive for.

Matthew 6:19–21 Lay not up for yourselves treasures upon earth, where moth and rust doth corrupt, and where thieves break through and steal: But lay up for yourselves treasures in heaven, where neither moth nor rust doth corrupt, and where thieves do not break through nor steal: For where your treasure is, there will your heart be also.

Notice also that Paul says he kept under his body, meaning he ran a controlled race, "not as one that beateth the air." He did not make any hasty decisions, but rather exercised self-discipline. He was patient, waiting for the right time to make his next move. He was careful to consult God on everything to be sure he did not waste any time, but rather spent it in the perfect will of God. He knew he ran his race for a heavenly reward that would never fade away. His greatest fear was to fail his heavenly Father, causing him to be put on the sideline (become a castaway) and not used again of God.

It should be our desire to run our Christian race as God directs us, but we must keep ourselves from sin to be the best spiritual athlete we can be.

Hebrews 12:1–3 Wherefore seeing we also are compassed about with so great a cloud of witnesses, let us lay aside every weight, and the sin which doth so easily beset us, and let us run with patience the race that is set before us, Looking unto Jesus the author and finisher of our faith; who for the joy that was set before him endured the cross, despising the shame, and is set down at the right hand of the throne of God. For consider him that endured such contradiction of sinners against himself, lest ye be wearied and faint in your minds.

As we race, our focus should be on Jesus. He ran His race on earth flawlessly and was not deterred by the circumstances around Him, even when He faced the cross, but counted it all joy. It pleased Him to please the Father.

We must lay sin to the side, realizing it can easily destroy our testimony and affect our race. In the book of Hebrews, Paul uses the analogy of a runner who removes any unnecessary weight that may slow him down and cause him to come short of the reward. Sin can interfere with our Christian life and limit our blessings from God. If not confessed and repented from, sin can remove us from the race entirely. There are others around us that depend on our Christian testimony, our witness, and our help to lead them to Christ. If we allow sin to defeat us, their souls may be at stake. Let us run our race with godly purpose and execution that, at the end, we may be able to say as Paul did;

2Timothy 4:6–8 For I am now ready to be offered, and the time of my departure is at hand. I have fought a good fight, I have finished my course, I have kept the faith: Henceforth there is laid up for me a crown of righteousness, which the Lord, the righteous judge, shall give me at that day: and not to me only, but unto all them also that love his appearing.

Preparing for the Christian race requires proper training and dedication, but there must also be a commitment. It is the commitment that will keep you in mind of why you are doing what you do and give justification to your actions. Training will equip you with knowledge and wisdom, and dedication will get you to church even on a cold morning, but commitment will keep you in God's service until He takes you to heaven.

Romans 12:1–2 I beseech you therefore, brethren, by the mercies of God, that ye present your bodies a living sacrifice, holy, acceptable unto God, which is your reasonable service. And be not conformed to this world: but be ye transformed by the renewing of your mind, that ye may prove what is that good, and acceptable, and perfect, will of God.

Let us look at these two verses a little closer. Paul addresses his audience as brethren. As a born-again Christian, you are a brother or sister to every other Christian, so you are part of the brethren. We have already seen that we have been adopted into God's family and are made joint heirs with Jesus Christ.

Next, he exhorts you to present your body. God cannot use inanimate objects to perform His work. Even angels do not have the privilege to witness to anyone or lead them to Christ. God uses Christian men, women, boys, and girls to carry out His salvation plan and purpose. He uses our lips to speak His word, our eyes to see those

29

in need, our ears to hear His still, small voice, our feet to carry the gospel, our hands to share with others, our minds to reason with others, our hearts to love others, and so on.

Your body is to be a living sacrifice. A dead body has no use on this earth, no matter who the body belonged to. Albert Einstein cannot quote any new formulas or revise any past theories from the grave, and we cannot serve God on this earth once we have passed from this life. We only have this life to give for our service to God, and we must make it count. In giving our life, it must be a sacrificial surrender. Just like the sacrificial animals in the Old Testament were submissive to the will of the priests, we must turn ourselves over completely to God's will for our life and let Him do with us as He determines best.

We should present ourselves holy and acceptable unto God. We know we are not perfect, and we never will be until we get to heaven. But we can ask God to help us to do our best to live a life that is pleasing to Him. Being holy means you are doing your best to fully obey God's word and, with the help of the Holy Spirit, you are keeping yourself from sin. Living a holy life will make you acceptable unto God and He will continue to use you in His service.

Presenting yourself unto God is your reasonable service. Making yourself available to God for His service is the minimum level of commitment to be expected from you. You may never be a preacher, a Sunday School teacher, missionary, or attain any church office, but you should at least be willing to serve in any capacity should God call you to it.

Verse two tells us that we should not be conformed, or made to look, talk, act, or dress like the world. Christians should be noticeably different in all these areas, and more. If you were to go on trial for being a Christian, the prosecuting attorney should not have to try very hard at all to convict you. You should stand out from the world, in a godly sense, and not blend in with it. We are to be transformed, or made different than we used to be, by renewing our mind. We are to strive for the mind of Christ that we might view things as He views them, and our purpose will be His purpose, that we will find ourselves in His perfect will for our life.

Running the Christian race does not happen by accident. It takes purposefully placed steps and sacrificed time to become what God has for you. The Holy Spirit will help you all the way, but no one will twist your arm to read your Bible, pray, go to church, or be a witness for Christ. You may have Christian friends who will encourage you to do these things, but they do not go home with you in the evening, they are not with you 24/7, and they cannot read your mind to know what you are really thinking. In other words, there are going to be many quiet times when it is only you and God alone. You must decide for yourself that when those quiet times come, and you even forget that God is still watching you, that you are going to encourage yourself to keep on keeping on. This is the commitment you must make on your own, that no matter what happens, you will not give up on God, and you will serve Him regardless of your circumstances. Remember, your circumstances do not make you who you are; it is how you respond to those circumstances.

As a Christian, you will have to arrange your priorities to place God first in your life if you want God's best for you. This does not mean your church attendance, your Christian ministries, or any other act of service. These are all good things, but they should not take the place or get in the way of your personal relationship with God. If you find that you are involved in so many activities that you have no time to build your spiritual life, then God would expect you to change something to get back on track.

You may ask, "If I put God before my family, won't that strain our family's relationship?" To answer this, keep two things in mind. One, when everyone in the family is right with God, they are right with each other. Two, if you put God first in your life, He will never ask you to place your family second. Building your relationship includes a personal prayer time, daily confessing your sins to God, reading your Bible for your own benefit and not just for a Sunday School lesson, allowing God to make changes in your physical life as He sees fit, and seeking His perfect will for your life.

A relationship typically takes time to develop while the participants learn about each other. God already knows everything about you, and you will learn about God by reading His Word, the Bible. As you discover God's character and allow Him to work in your life, your relationship with Him will grow deeper and more meaningful.

The bottom line is that you must make a commitment to serve the Lord. A half-hearted dedication or infrequent Bible study or church attendance will not get the job done. Letting God have your left-over time may make you feel like you are doing Him a service, but He knows the difference. Make it a point to find the time to make a life-long commitment to serve God. Commit your time to read and study His word, to pray every day, to faithfully attend church, and to be a witness. Commit your finances to support your local church and to keep its ministries in operation. Commit your talents to serve in your church as best you can.

As you can see, accepting Christ as your personal Savior is only the beginning of your Christian life. God does not expect you to sit on the fence and watch time go by while others die and go to hell. There is a reason God did not strike you dead and take you to heaven immediately after you got saved. He has a purpose for your life that has not been completed yet. It is your responsibility to seek that purpose and, when you have found it, perform it willingly.

Your race began the moment you got saved. As a child of God, your first act of obedience is to be baptized. Baptism does not wash away your sins or make you any more fit for heaven than shaving your head, but it demonstrates to those who witness it what you believe in your heart. Jesus was baptized in the Jordan River by John the Baptist to show others He identified with, and gave approval to, the message John preached to the people— that Jesus was the Messiah. The baptism of Jesus shows it plays no part in salvation; as Jesus did not need to get saved. It is an act of obedience by those who have been saved.

Baptism is the one thing that separates most religions. It is biblical that baptism follows salvation, though others may mistakenly preach that it is an essential part of salvation. When the Pharisees came to John the Baptist to be baptized in the Jordan river, he would not allow anyone that had not repented from their sins. In the book of Acts, the following is recorded as another example that baptism is not something done on a whim.

Acts 8:26–39 And the angel of the Lord spake unto Philip, saying, Arise, and go toward the south unto the way that goeth down from Jerusalem unto Gaza, which is desert. And he arose and went: and, behold, a man of Ethiopia, an eunuch of great authority under Candace queen of the Ethiopians, who had the charge of all her treasure, and had come to Jerusalem for to worship, Was returning, and sitting in his chariot read Isaiah the prophet. Then the Spirit said unto Philip, Go near, and join thyself to this chariot. And Philip ran thither to him, and heard him read the prophet Isaiah, and said, Understandest thou what thou readest? And he said, How can I, except some man should guide me? And he desired Philip that he would come up and sit with him. The place of the Scripture which he read was this, He was led as a sheep to the slaughter; and like a lamb dumb before his shearer, so opened he not his mouth: In his humiliation his judgment was taken away: and who shall declare his generation? for his life is taken from the earth. And the eunuch answered Philip, and said, I pray thee, of whom speaketh the prophet this? of himself, or of some other man? Then Philip opened his mouth, and began at the same Scripture, and preached unto him Jesus. And as they went on their way, they came unto a certain water: and the eunuch said, See, here is water; what doth hinder me to be baptized? And Philip said, If thou believest with all thine heart, thou mayest. And he answered and said, I believe that Jesus Christ is the Son of God. And he commanded the chariot to stand still: and they went down both into the water, both Philip and the eunuch; and he baptized him. And when they

34

were come up out of the water, the Spirit of the
Lord caught away Philip, that the eunuch saw him
no more: and he went on his way rejoicing.

So, we see that baptism follows salvation. Also note
that both, Philip and the eunuch, went into the water. That
is, Philip properly baptized the eunuch by fully immersing
him in the water to symbolically illustrate that the eunuch's
old man was buried, and the new man was resurrected to
new life to serve God. After all, dead people are not
sprinkled with dirt, but fully buried. The eunuch was not
sprinkled with water, but his whole body was fully
immersed.

Note that had Philip not obeyed the angel of God (vs.
26), the eunuch may have not gotten saved. Philip had
made a commitment to serve God and was immediately
available when He called. In verse 36 the eunuch requested
baptism and Philip responded in verse 37 that it was only
possible if the eunuch accepted Jesus as his Savior, which
he did.

Your spiritual life will progress as you study your Bible.

2Timothy 2:15 Study to show thyself approved
unto God, a workman that needeth not to be
ashamed, rightly dividing the word of truth.

1Peter 2:2 As newborn babes, desire the sincere
milk of the word, that ye may grow thereby:

You are God's workman employed in His service, so
you need to learn all you can, which will enable you to
correctly understand the Word of God and apply it to your
everyday life. As you continue to study and gain wisdom,
you will go beyond the "sincere milk of the word" (basic

doctrines) to the meat of the word (life applications, help for counseling others, understanding deeper doctrines, etc.).

1Peter 3:15 But sanctify the Lord God in your hearts: and be ready always to give an answer to every man that asketh you a reason of the hope that is in you with meekness and fear:

You will find that the Bible speaks to the deepest recesses of the heart and will convict of sin.

Hebrews 4:12 For the word of God is quick, and powerful, and sharper than any two-edged sword, piercing even to the dividing asunder of soul and spirit, and of the joints and marrow, and is a discerner of the thoughts and intents of the heart.

Quick, in this verse, means the word of God is alive, not dead. It is dynamic in the sense that it can apply to every individual in their own unique circumstances and has been, is, and will be, applicable to all spans of time. The Bible is not an antiquated collection of men's stories from the past. It is the Word of God, penned by men as they were moved by the Holy Spirit of God.

2Peter 1:21 For the prophecy came not in old time by the will of man: but holy men of God spake as they were moved by the Holy Ghost.

Nothing in the Bible was written by accident or without purpose.

The word of God is also powerful. It brings families together where social programs fail by explaining the different roles of family members and encouraging them to love one another. It gives hope to the downtrodden, that God has not forgotten them. It mends old, emotional wounds and scars of the repentant. It will give life instructions to anyone who reads it. It reveals God to us in a very personal way that we may know Him more intimately.

The phrase, "sharper than any two-edged sword", reveals that the word of God has a deep convicting power that penetrates our deepest recesses, yet it does not leave a physical mark on you. The Bible reveals our shortcomings and humbles us, so we do not generate a sinful, proud spirit. The more we read, the more we realize how sinful we really are, unable and unworthy to stand before a holy and righteous God without our Savior, Jesus Christ. Our sins are laid out before us like a blanket spread for a picnic, that we might confess them to God and turn from them. Even our wicked thoughts are penetrated by the word of God, and we are unable to hide them from its illumination. The Bible is a soul-cleansing agent, but we must heed to its conviction and repent from our sins to make it useful.

Bible study is important to your progression in the Christian faith. Learn the Bible, grow as a Christian, learn Bible doctrine, live for God, have a testimony, witness to others, participate in church activities, teach others, pray for yourself and others.

1Timothy 2:1–3 I exhort therefore, that, first of all, supplications, prayers, intercessions, and giving of thanks, be made for all men; For kings, and for all that are in authority; that we may lead a quiet and peaceable life in all godliness and honesty. For this is good and acceptable in the sight of God our Savior;

Spread the gospel.

Acts 5:42 And daily in the temple, and in every house, they ceased not to teach and preach Jesus Christ.

The early Christians did not have the Bible (New Testament) but were eyewitnesses to many of the things recorded therein. As they moved throughout the geographical area, they carried these experiences with them, along with the message of the Savior Who would save anyone that called upon His name. They needed no script to follow to witness to unbelievers; they simply told what they knew about what had taken place in their own lives. The gospel is just too good to hold back and not share with others.

As evidenced by the early Christians, you do not have to be a theologian to speak to someone about Jesus; just tell what happened to you. Rehearse your testimony of salvation and the events that drew you to make the most important decision of your life. Tell how God has changed your life since you accepted Christ as your savior. Teach others what God has taught you from His Word.

Do not let others intimidate you by keeping you from proclaiming God's good news. You will be mocked and ridiculed for taking a stand for Christ but think of what He has done for you!

Romans 1:16 For I am not ashamed of the gospel of Christ: for it is the power of God unto salvation to every one that believeth; to the Jew first, and also to the Greek.

2Timothy 1:7 For God hath not given us the spirit of fear; but of power, and of love, and of a sound mind.

Hebrews 13:6 So that we may boldly say, The Lord is my helper, and I will not fear what man shall do unto me.

In the book of Matthew, chapter 10, when Jesus sent His disciples preaching, He commanded they fear no one, but rely on the strength and provision of the Heavenly Father. No other human has power over your soul, nor does anyone else possess the ability to influence your soul's disposition. Your eternal abode was settled the moment you accepted Christ as your Savior, and no man is going to change that!

Matthew 10:28 And fear not them which kill the body, but are not able to kill the soul: but rather fear him which is able to destroy both soul and body in hell.

Do not give up. Remember, you made a commitment to finish the race. Others are watching you run and depend on you staying faithful and true all the way to your respective finish. You may be the only Christian some people will ever meet, and, if you show them a consistent life, you may lead some of them to Christ.

Galations 6:9 And let us not be weary in well doing: for in due season we shall reap, if we faint not.

Times can, and will, get hard, but Jesus is the All-Sufficient One that can make us overcomers, because He has overcome the world.

John 16:33 These things I have spoken unto you, that in me ye might have peace. In the world ye shall have tribulation: but be of good cheer; I have overcome the world.

Satan will try to pull you down, but you belong to the omnipotent God of heaven.

1John 4:4 Ye are of God, little children, and have overcome them: because greater is he that is in you, than he that is in the world.

Temptations will come, but stand firm. We have God's promise that He will help us through them all. In the beginning of Jesus' ministry, Satan presented Him with every temptation known to man—the pride of life, the lust of the flesh, and the lust of the eyes. Jesus was able to overcome each of these temptations with the Word of God, and that is how we will be able to do the same.

As the following verse states, God knows our individual limit for temptation and will not allow us to be overburdened. If we give in to temptation, it is not God's fault for letting us fall, it is our fault for not letting Him help us. When the load is too heavy to bear, call unto God for help, and He will help us to bear it.

1Corinthians 10:13 There hath no temptation taken you but such as is common to man: but God is faithful, who will not suffer you to be tempted above that ye are able; but will with the temptation also make a way to escape, that ye may be able to bear it.

Recognize that the Christian life is not a bed of roses. As stated before, tribulations, trials, and temptations will come, and you decide how you will react to them. You may be hampered with a physical malady as was the Apostle Paul, but, like Paul, you can claim God's grace and continue to serve Him despite your imposition. Paul said he prayed three times for God to take away his "thorn in the flesh" but God's response was sufficient.

2Corinthians 12:9 And he said unto me, My grace is sufficient for thee: for my strength is made perfect in weakness. Most gladly therefore will I rather glory in my infirmities, that the power of Christ may rest upon me.

The race we run is one against time. Someday God will bring an end to all time and will usher in eternity, and there will be no second chance for those who are not saved. No one knows when that will be, not even Jesus.

Mark 13:32 But of that day and that hour knoweth no man, no, not the angels which are in heaven, neither the Son, but the Father.

As well, no man knows when his last day of life will be on earth, so it is just as imperative that the Christian use his time wisely as a witness for Christ. How hard would we work for God if we knew the hour of our death? How much harder should we work for Him knowing our death could be at any moment?

Ephesians 5:15–17 See then that ye walk circumspectly, not as fools, but as wise, Redeeming the time, because the days are evil. Wherefore be ye not unwise, but understanding what the will of the Lord is.

Our race is also a spiritual battle, and we must be prepared to war against our enemy, Satan. We are in the Lord's army, and there is no discharge. The following section from the book of Ephesians describes how we are to arm ourselves with the Word of God.

Ephesians 6:10–18 Finally, my brethren, be strong in the Lord, and in the power of his might. Put on the whole armor of God, that ye may be able to stand against the wiles of the devil. For we wrestle not against flesh and blood, but against principalities, against powers, against the rulers of the darkness of this world, against spiritual wickedness in high places. Wherefore take unto you the whole armor of God, that ye may be able to withstand in the evil day, and having done all, to stand. Stand therefore, having your loins girt about with truth, and having on the breastplate of righteousness; And your feet shod with the preparation of the gospel of peace; Above all, taking the shield of faith, wherewith ye shall be able to quench all the fiery darts of the wicked. And take the helmet of salvation, and the sword of the Spirit, which is the word of God: Praying always with all prayer and supplication in the Spirit, and watching thereunto with all perseverance and supplication for all saints;

Keep your eye on the prize. We know heaven awaits all believers, but there is little information in the Bible about what we will be doing for eternity. Some think heaven will grow boring after a time; I think not. God will have a position for each of us, and we will serve Him with a glad heart. Regardless of what our individual responsibilities will be, no Christian would trade their assignment for even a moment in hell. We can try to imagine what God has for

us, but our human intellect is very limited All we know is
that it will be glorious and wonderful.

> *1 Corinthians 2:9 But as it is written, Eye hath not
> seen, nor ear heard, neither have entered into the
> heart of man, the things which God hath prepared
> for them that love him.*

WHO IS SATAN?

Satan is one of God's created beings. He was one of the most beautiful creatures and evidently had a special part in the affairs of heaven as the covering cherub. The book of Ezekiel gives a short synopsis of his beginning and his fall in the following excerpt, though it is addressed to the king of Tyrus.

Ezekiel 28:12–17 Son of man, take up a lamentation upon the king of Tyrus, and say unto him, Thus saith the Lord GOD; Thou sealest up the sum, full of wisdom, and perfect in beauty. Thou hast been in Eden the garden of God; every precious stone was thy covering, the sardius, topaz, and the diamond, the beryl, the onyx, and the jasper, the sapphire, the emerald, and the carbuncle, and gold: the workmanship of thy tabrets and of thy pipes was prepared in thee in the day that thou wast created. Thou art the anointed cherub that covereth; and I have set thee so: thou wast upon the holy mountain of God; thou hast walked up and down in the midst of the stones of fire. Thou wast perfect in thy ways from the day that thou wast created, till iniquity was found in thee. By the multitude of thy merchandise they have filled the midst of thee with violence, and thou hast sinned: therefore I will cast thee as profane out of the mountain of God: and I will destroy thee, O covering cherub, from the midst of the stones of fire. Thine heart was lifted up because of thy beauty, thou hast corrupted thy wisdom by reason of thy brightness: I will cast thee to the ground, I will lay thee before kings, that they may behold thee.

In the book of John, Jesus gave a short summation of Satan while He spoke point-blank to some rebellious Pharisees who resisted the truth.

John 8:44 Ye are of your father the devil, and the lusts of your father ye will do. He was a murderer from the beginning, and abode not in the truth, because there is no truth in him. When he speaketh a lie, he speaketh of his own: for he is a liar, and the father of it.

Our introduction to Satan in scripture is in the Garden of Eden, in the book of Genesis, chapter 3. At this time, there were only two people in the world, Adam and Eve, and they existed in a perfect environment free from sin. They knew no evil, only good. The Garden of Eden contained all manner of trees and plants that God had made for man to enjoy, and Adam's job was to care for it. God told Adam and Eve they were free to eat of any tree in the Garden, but they were forbidden to eat from the tree of knowledge of good and evil.

In Genesis 3:1, Satan appears to Eve in the form of a serpent and convinces her to eat of the forbidden tree. The

Bible says she gave the fruit unto Adam, and he ate also. Their eyes were opened to understand good and evil, and sin entered their lives because of their disobedience. God expelled them from the Garden, and Adam's sin has passed on to every generation since.

Romans 5:12 Wherefore, as by one man sin entered into the world, and death by sin; and so death passed upon all men, for that all have sinned:

Satan was successful getting man to fall from God's grace to a sinful condition. Now, everyone has the penalty of sin on their life that must be dealt with, a price that must be paid, a price which we cannot pay.

As addressed in the book of Isaiah, Satan's downfall began with his pride. He had exalted himself to the point where he thought he could be higher and mightier than God, and he convinced a large number of angels to go along with him—he failed. God cast Satan from heaven, along with the fallen angels, destined for eventual condemnation in the Lake of Fire for eternity. We do not know exactly when Satan rebelled, but he appeared early in the Garden of Eden, as accounted above. It seems that as soon as God had finished His creation on earth, Satan was there to try to destroy it.

Isaiah 14:12–14 How art thou fallen from heaven, O Lucifer, son of the morning! how art thou cut down to the ground, which didst weaken the nations! For thou hast said in thine heart, I will ascend into heaven, I will exalt my throne above the stars of God: I will sit also upon the mount of the congregation, in the sides of the north: I will

47

ascend above the heights of the clouds; I will be like the most High.

We would be foolish to discount the existence of Satan and the role he plays in the world today. His influence covers the full spectrum of ungodly works; from the murderous atrocities we hear of around the world that make us cringe, to the subtle nuances that guide men's hearts everywhere to sin. He is the enemy of God, whose ultimate goal is to destroy God's plan for mankind's redemption. He is very powerful—though he can do nothing without God's permission—and has a host of wicked demons that follow and obey him. He uses his power to sway the minds and hearts of people, to guide them in all manner of ungodliness to destroy lives.

Though Satan was cast from heaven, he evidently still retains the privilege of going before God to accuse believers, as the Bible tells us he is there accusing day and night. It was on one such occasion that Satan accused Job, an Old Testament saint written about in the book of the Bible that bears his name. Satan accused Job of having life too easy, that he was a happy man that honored God because he had all the material possessions of life, not realizing Job put his trust in God, not in what he owned. Knowing what kind of man Job was, God gave Satan permission to strike at Job, but not to take his life. Through a series of catastrophes, Satan took all that Job had; his ten children, thousands of animals, and many servants, leaving his wife only. The Bible records Job's response.

Job 1:21–22 And said, Naked came I out of my mother's womb, and naked shall I return thither: the LORD gave, and the LORD hath taken away;

blessed be the name of the LORD. In all this Job
sinned not, nor charged God foolishly.

As the previous example helps illustrate, there is a battle that rages on continuously over the souls of men and women; God wants to claim and take them to heaven; Satan desires to take them to hell. Satan knows that once we belong to God, he cannot claim us for his own, but he tries his best to disrupt our Christian walk and minimize our positive impact on others to accept Christ. He and his demons work constantly to keep unbelievers from coming to the saving knowledge of Jesus Christ. He hides the gospel from them, he occupies their time to keep them from church, and he promises to supply them every lust imaginable to dismiss any serious thoughts of eternity. Job's life not only demonstrated that Satan's actions can affect us physically, but also shows this is a battle fought on a spiritual level.

Ephesians 6:12 For we wrestle not against flesh and blood, but against principalities, against powers, against the rulers of the darkness of this world, against spiritual wickedness in high places.

2Corinthians 4:3–4 But if our gospel be hid, it is hid to them that are lost: In whom the god of this world hath blinded the minds of them which believe not, lest the light of the glorious gospel of Christ, who is the image of God, should shine unto them.

Today, Jesus serves as our advocate with the Father to defend us against Satan's accusations and attacks. He intercedes on our behalf to claim us for His own and to protect us from the tempter's snare and condemnation.

49

Romans 8:34 Who is he that condemneth? It is Christ that died, yea rather, that is risen again, who is even at the right hand of God, who also maketh intercession for us.

1Timothy 2:5 For there is one God, and one mediator between God and men, the man Christ Jesus;

1John 2:1 My little children, these things write I unto you, that ye sin not. And if any man sin, we have an advocate with the Father, Jesus Christ the righteous:

We must respect the power of Satan and his underworld, but we do not have to fear it, as he can do nothing against us without God's permission. Our human flesh is no match against his strength and wisdom, so we must let Jesus fight these battles for us.

1John 4:4 Ye are of God, little children, and have overcome them: because greater is he that is in you, than he that is in the world.

Use the Word of God to proclaim the name of Jesus, which has power to cause demons to flee. Do not let Satan get a foothold in your life. He is looking for any opportunity to destroy you, your Christian testimony, or both.

Ephesians 4:27 Neither give place to the devil.

1Peter 5:8 Be sober, be vigilant; because your adversary the devil, as a roaring lion, walketh about, seeking whom he may devour:

James 4:7 Submit yourselves therefore to God. Resist the devil, and he will flee from you.

Claim the blood of Jesus that has washed you of your sins and justifies you as one of His.

Romans 5:9 Much more then, being now justified by his blood, we shall be saved from wrath through him.

Ephesians 1:7 In whom we have redemption through his blood, the forgiveness of sins, according to the riches of his grace;

Satan desires to control your mind. Even if you are a Christian, if he can control your mind, he can lead you away from serving God and make you an ineffective witness for Christ. This would make it very difficult for you to convince anyone to go to church with you—much less hear your testimony—if you do not live a consistent Christian life. As we said before, living the Christian life is not a bed of roses. It takes purposeful effort—not to remain saved—to live a consistent and faithful life and to maintain a strong testimony for Christ. This often means going through some tribulation and trials, but souls are in the balance.

Though Satan is very powerful, we must remember that he is a created being and subject to the authority of God. Many instances are recorded in the New Testament of people possessed with demons, who were set free at the command of Jesus. Demons have no choice when Jesus speaks but to follow His every command. The following is just one example.

Matthew 9:32–33 As they went out, behold, they brought to him a dumb man possessed with a devil. And when the devil was cast out, the dumb spake: and the multitudes marveled, saying, It was never so seen in Israel.

The book of Revelation shows Satan's end recorded in two instances that will transpire in the future. The first is when Satan is cast out of heaven for good, never allowed to go back. Note the many names used to denote him.

Revelation 12:9–10 And the great dragon was cast out, that old serpent, called the Devil, and Satan, which deceiveth the whole world: he was cast out into the earth, and his angels were cast out with him. And I heard a loud voice saying in heaven, Now is come salvation, and strength, and the kingdom of our God, and the power of his Christ: for the accuser of our brethren is cast down, which accused them before our God day and night.

The second instance is when Satan is delivered to his eternal abode.

Revelation 20:10 And the devil that deceived them was cast into the lake of fire and brimstone, where the beast and the false prophet are, and shall be tormented day and night forever and ever.

WHAT IS SIN?

Imagine a country with no laws. "Absurd!" you say? What if every citizen of this mythical country always did what was right, looked after each other's best interest, and never sought to defraud or harm anyone? If there were such a country, and there is not, it would have no need for laws. As the Bible tells us, laws are not for the obedient, but for the disobedient.

> *1 Timothy 1:9–11 Knowing this, that the law is not made for a righteous man, but for the lawless and disobedient, for the ungodly and for sinners, for unholy and profane, for murderers of fathers and murderers of mothers, for manslayers, For whoremongers, for them that defile themselves with mankind, for menstealers, for liars, for perjured persons, and if there be any other thing that is contrary to sound doctrine; According to the glorious gospel of the blessed God, which was committed to my trust.*

If you have never broken the law, you would probably categorize yourself as a law-abiding citizen. You are the kind of person that can get by without having to know what the law says, because you never do anything to violate it. In other words, your normal, everyday routine naturally keeps you out of trouble. This may make you an ideal citizen and respectful member of your community, but have you broken God's law? Think about the following summation of God's law.

Galatians 5:14 For all the law is fulfilled in one word, even in this; Thou shalt love thy neighbour as thyself.

This verse is not talking about the person necessarily living next door or in the same apartment complex, but anyone you encounter. We are to treat everyone as our neighbor and love them as we love ourselves. Sound impossible? It is! I am sure there are names and faces flashing through your mind even now of those you have mistreated, mocked, abused, spoke unkindly to, lied to, etc. All of us have violated God's law.

Romans 3:10 As it is written, There is none righteous, no, not one:

Even our best attempt at a clean life is not good enough.

Isaiah 64:6 But we are all as an unclean thing, and all our righteousnesses are as filthy rags; and we all do fade as a leaf; and our iniquities, like the wind, have taken us away.

Sin is the violation of God's law, and only one sin makes us guilty.

1 John 3:4 Whosoever committeth sin transgresseth also the law: for sin is the transgression of the law.

Romans 3:23 For all have sinned, and come short of the glory of God;

No one can escape the power of sin in their own strength. It slips into our lives slowly, a little at a time, and becomes the master of those who allow it to control them. As young children, most of us probably lied at least once to our parents. If not corrected early, lying may continue into your adolescence and adulthood years. What about that first drink, smoke, illegal drug, or ungodly relationship. If these are not dealt with in their infancy, they may be the first of many to come. But sin is not just the really bad things we hear of: robbing, smoking, drinking, killing, stealing, ungodly sexual acts, etc. It also includes the simple things like lying to your children, not keeping a promise, wasting time at work, fudging on your taxes, etc. Man classifies sin as big and little, but God does not. Man will excuse small sins, God will not. To God, sin is sin, regardless of what act it is.

Sin is contagious. It seems when someone figures out how to steal money an easier way, a line forms with those who are willing to give it a try. Copycats spring up all the time to imitate all manner of illegal and ungodly acts. Even young children usually find it easier to imitate bad behavior than good, often laughed at by parents as something that is cute or adorable. If you have young children and you allow bad behavior, ask yourself, "Do I want my child to behave like this when they are sixteen?" If your answer is, "No," then help stop the infectious spread.

As well, sin can be addictive (just ask any chain smoker or alcoholic) and it can include any sin. Telling lies can become so habitual, friends and family eventually start expecting you to lie to them. Taking that extra ten-minute break at work can become a normal part of your every workday. Take things from work often enough, and you will start scratching things off your personal department-store shopping list, knowing you will get them at the office.

Sin does not have to be chemically dependent, as usually associated with drugs and alcohol, but can be just as addictive. When we repeat the same offense repeatedly, our senses become dull to the wrongful nature of it, and the act eventually becomes an acceptable practice, to which we give no second thought to performing.

It is a lie to say that no one enjoys sin; that is what makes it so appealing to the flesh. The Bible says everything the world has to offer us is geared for the flesh.

1 John 2:16 For all that is in the world, the lust of the flesh, and the lust of the eyes, and the pride of life, is not of the Father, but is of the world.

We all have God-given, inward desires and an urge to have them satisfied, but there is a right way and a wrong way to satisfy them. A sin is committed when we satisfy a God-given desire in a God-forbidden way. For example, you may need fifty dollars to pay an honest debt, but stealing the money is not God's way to take care of it.

Part of the illusion of sin being good for us is that it seems to give us control over our life. And who does not like to be in control of satisfying their own desires? There is something about taking control of our lives and exercising that control by giving ourselves things that we know are forbidden by our parents and other authority figures, even things expressly forbidden by God. Our intent is to never go too far, but sometimes too far is where we end up. There is a song by Harold McWhorter (Sin Will Take You Farther) that says,

"Sin will take you farther than you want to go, slowly but wholly taking control. Sin will leave you longer than you want to stay. Sin will cost you far more than you want to pay."

How true that is. Just ask anyone who has taken the path of sin for any length of time at all; eventually, everyone wants off, but some find out too late.

Sin has become very subjective. We have white lies, gray areas, and situation ethics. To the world, the result decides whether an action is a sin or not. If lying to your friend spares their feelings, then it is okay. If you steal only when you must, then no harm is done. Lying to a police officer to keep from getting a ticket does not hurt anyone, does it? Nothing is right or wrong in these instances; it all depends on the circumstances and the outcome. This is man's thinking.

This mindset has crept into our classrooms, as kids are instructed that there are no underachievers; everyone is a winner. Test answers are no longer black or white, right or wrong. The final grade depends on what you think of your own progress and self-worth. If you were challenged by the class project and you did your best, you get an A; forget that you did not do any of the required paperwork. What are these people going to do when they hit the business world and get told they need to step it up, they are not cutting it, they are not catching on, or they are fired? What happened to making kids work for the result and being responsible for their own failure?

> *Isaiah 5:20 Woe unto them that call evil good, and good evil; that put darkness for light, and light for darkness; that put bitter for sweet, and sweet for bitter!*

Sin is all Satan has to offer us, but we often easily accept it.

Since God is holy and righteous, and will not be in the presence of sin, our sin will keep us from His presence—now and for eternity—unless it is properly dealt with. Only Christ offers a solution.

WHAT IS A CHRISTIAN?

Today, many have their own idea of what a Christian is. Someone born in a country characterized as Christian. Someone who has compassion for their fellow mankind. Anyone born in the United States. Anyone who expresses any general concept of Christian-like behavior. Anyone who believes in a god, or supernatural power. Anyone born to Christian parents.

If any of these definitions were true, there would be Christians in every nation and tribe around the world, totaling at least in the hundreds of millions, if not billions of people. Try to imagine anyone you know who would be left off the list if all the above statements were true. Stalin and Hitler come to mind, but who knows. Maybe they had even shown compassion to at least one person in their respective lifetimes. It seems absurd to think just anyone can be labeled as a Christian simply because of the good acts, or lack of bad acts, in their life. But no one is a Christian because of birthright, belief, or benefit of being labeled as such. You may carry the name, but God knows whose His are, and who are imposters.

There are a lot of people in the world that get characterized as good based on what we know about them. If we see they have a decent moral foundation and they don't drink or smoke, we might mistakenly believe God sees them as good people, based on their lifestyle. If they have never been in trouble with the law or abused their family, if they go to church with any frequency at all, we automatically label them as Christians. The coworker who doesn't go drinking with the others is the goody two-shoes everyone just knows is going to heaven. The neighbor who does not like rock-and-roll music, immodest dress, or filthy language is candidly referred to by the community as the neighborhood preacher, whether he goes to church or not.

Many times, the elderly are viewed in such a compassionate light that they are all sweet and kind by the time of their death, intimating they all go to heaven. At the time of Yasir Arafat's death in 2004, the world media fell at his feet, portraying him as a kind, gentle grandfather, forgiving his terroristic and murderous past, all because he was old and ill. They were willing to look the other way and give him a free pass to paradise. Others who have lost their battle with a long-term or painful illness are virtually ushered into heaven upon their death by those left behind, assuming their time of suffering is over—is it? Man's judgment of what is good, much less Christian, is not always correct.

Being labeled as a Christian does not transform anyone into a Christian no more than being labeled a lawyer will transform a monkey into a lawyer. Labels and titles are usually earned or granted by higher authority, not bought or assumed by people desiring them. Someone who falsely wears a title may someday be asked to present the credentials to prove their identity. What would you use as evidence to prove you are a Christian? Hopefully you have witnesses you could call to tell of the positive changes they have seen in your life since your decision to follow Christ; changes they know had to start on the inside; changes that would be characteristic of Christ. Does a label make these things happen? On the contrary, it is the demonstration of the changes that bring about the label. Wearing a name does not change the heart of an individual, but when Jesus changes the heart, the individual has a new name to wear.

After Jesus ascended to heaven, the disciples found themselves almost in a state of limbo, not sure what to do next. They knew they could no longer worship as the other Jews in the area, observing the law and the priesthood and awaiting the Messiah; for the Messiah had come, even though the other Jews did not believe Jesus was the One. They also knew they could not pretend nothing had happened, as Jesus had touched their lives, and they would never be the same again. Following Jesus' command, they banded together to wait for the promise of the Comforter, as recorded in the book of Acts, chapter 2.

Acts 2:1–4 And when the day of Pentecost was fully come, they were all with one accord in one place. And suddenly there came a sound from heaven as of a rushing mighty wind, and it filled all the house where they were sitting. And there appeared unto them cloven tongues like as of fire, and it sat upon each of them. And they were all filled with the Holy Ghost, and began to speak with other tongues, as the Spirit gave them utterance.

The indwelling of the Holy Spirit changed everything for the believers that day. They now had Someone to lead and guide them and give them wisdom and direction for their lives in relation to God's will for each of them. They suddenly found themselves full of courage and boldness to preach the message of Christ to all who would listen and assemble as groups of believers at regular and frequent intervals. They now had a new mission—take the gospel of Christ to every nation on earth.

Matthew 28:19–20 Go ye therefore, and teach all nations, baptizing them in the name of the Father, and of the Son, and of the Holy Ghost: Teaching them to observe all things whatsoever I have commanded you: and, lo, I am with you always, even unto the end of the world.

This new mission brought on a new name. The Bible says the disciples were called Christians first at the Church in Antioch (Acts 11:26). The term was originally used to mock those who displayed actions as followers of Christ. These believers were recognized by their communities as having a different walk and a different talk from others in the area, reminiscent of what they had seen and heard in Jesus. They preached a new message of the resurrected Christ and how anyone could trust in His name to secure their individual place in heaven. They carried this message with passion and proclaimed no substitution for those wishing to avoid eternal condemnation.

Though many may call themselves Christian today, whether because of tradition, association, or affiliation, most are not. The definition adopted by the world has become so diluted and encompassing over the centuries, it seems as though it is easier to believe an unbeliever is a Christian than it is to prove he is not, as almost anything qualifies. How sad! This is what Jesus had to say about these Christian imposters.

Matthew 7:21–23 Not every one that saith unto me, Lord, Lord, shall enter into the kingdom of heaven; but he that doeth the will of my Father which is in heaven. Many will say to me in that day, Lord, Lord, have we not prophesied in thy name and in thy name have cast out devils? and in thy name done many wonderful works? And then will I profess unto them, I never knew you: depart from me, ye that work iniquity.

Registering for a nametag at the front door for an antique convention may get you in the show, but there is no place to register at the gates of heaven to enter there. Death is too late! Your decision to become a Christian is made in this life, and it is not one to be made lightly. There must be a change in the heart, the emotional seat of your being, a desire to follow Christ. There must be a confession to God of what you believe about Jesus. There must be a call unto God to request His salvation.

Even in the early Church, the name Christian became the well-known, accepted title for all who had placed their faith in Jesus Christ, and Him only. Believers gladly wore the title for the Savior, even in the face of persecution. The Apostle Peter wrote;

1Peter 4:16 Yet if any man suffer as a Christian, let him not be ashamed; but let him glorify God on this behalf.

In the book of Acts, chapter 21, the unbelieving Jews were successful at having the Apostle Paul falsely arrested for crimes they could not prove. In the days to follow, he would give his defense before several dignitaries, one of which was King Agrippa. Paul rehearsed with the king the history of the Jewish people and the promises God had made concerning the Messiah and argued that the promises had now been fulfilled in Jesus Christ. He testified of his own conversion and how Jesus had transformed him from a persecutor to a preacher. Though Paul had not used the word Christian in his testimony, the king easily recognized the subject of discussion.

Acts 26:28 Then Agrippa said unto Paul, Almost thou persuadest me to be a Christian.

The king knew it was open for anyone to become a Christian, but it took a personal act of repentance to be able to wear the name, and he was not ready to make that commitment. It was well known then that all who had trusted in Jesus were called Christians by the world, and only those who had trusted in Jesus called themselves Christians. Unbelievers refused to take the name, recognizing its connection with the Son of God and the political persecution that often accompanied it. Today, people will wear the name Christian as casually as the latest clothing fad, without fully understanding either.

Becoming a Christian is a conscious individual decision to accept Chris as your personal Savior. No one can make the decision for you, and you cannot make it for anyone else. You cannot sit idly by and expect this life-altering, eternity-changing event to occur automatically without your involvement. Not making a decision is the same as deciding to reject Christ; a decision you will eternally regret.

Becoming a Christian is not a matter of how well you know the Bible; rather, how well you know you are a sinner. A Christian is a sinner saved by God's grace.

WHAT IS SALVATION?

Salvation is God's act of grace in response to our penitent plea for mercy from the judgment of our sin, which changes our eternal destination from hell to heaven. It is the act of saving one from eternal damnation; thus, those who have received salvation have been saved, or rescued, from eternal condemnation. When someone receives salvation, they no longer need to worry about being condemned to hell once they die, for they have escaped this judgment and have been given a new home in heaven that awaits them. Our heavenly position is so sure, it is as though we are seated in heaven right now.

Ephesians 2:6 And hath raised us up together, and made us sit together in heavenly places in Christ Jesus:

Each of us is born in sin with our soul already condemned and on our way to hell upon our physical death. Our sin debt must be paid to redeem our soul for us to go to heaven. But this debt requires a sinless sacrifice. Since we are all born in sin, no human can satisfy the qualifications and there is no manner of works that we can perform as a substitute.

Ephesians 2:8–9 For by grace are ye saved through faith; and that not of yourselves: it is the gift of God: Not of works, lest any man should boast.

Our sin has earned us death; not just physical death of the body but also eternal death of our soul and spirit in hell. To prevent this, we can accept God's free gift of salvation and receive life eternal.

Romans 6:23 For the wages of sin is death; but the gift of God is eternal life through Jesus Christ our Lord.

It is only by the mercy of God that we are given an opportunity to accept Jesus as our Savior, and it is His grace that bestows salvation unto us.

Salvation is not an act that can be witnessed like a double play in a baseball game, though the results are quite evident. Jesus explained it to a man in the Bible named Nicodemus with an illustration.

John 3:8 The wind bloweth where it listeth, and thou hearest the sound thereof, but canst not tell whence it cometh, and whither it goeth: so is every one that is born of the Spirit.

Salvation is a spiritual matter that takes place in the heart of the new believer, unable to be physically viewed by anyone else. In our baseball example, imagine a player on first base and his teammate comes up to bat with one out in the inning. If the television went off just as the player swung his bat and came back on after the double play was completed, you would not know the details of what had just happened, but the actions on the field would confirm what the sportscasters were telling you. Similarly, the wind cannot be viewed, but we can see the effects of the wind as it blows the leaves, bends the tree limbs, etc. So, we cannot literally see the instantaneous transformation that takes place in a person's heart when he gets saved, but we can see the positive changes in attitude, actions, and habits that salvation brings over time into one's life.

Salvation is an immediate and spontaneous response to our repentance of sin and call upon God to save us. If we are sincere in our desire to be saved, God does not withhold His grace from us, but bestows it upon us without hesitation. Even before you utter the request to God, He already knows you have repented in your heart.

Romans 10:9–10 That if thou shalt confess with thy mouth the Lord Jesus, and shalt believe in thine heart that God hath raised him from the dead, thou shalt be saved. For with the heart man believeth unto righteousness; and with the mouth confession is made unto salvation.

Though he knows we are sinful and far from perfect, He gives us His free gift and begins a new work in us to mold us to the image of His Son, Jesus Christ.

Philippians 1:6 Being confident of this very thing, that he which hath begun a good work in you will perform it until the day of Jesus Christ:

This new work begins the very moment we are saved and is not over until our death, after which we enter our new eternal abode in heaven. Though our eternal destination is settled the very instant God sends His Spirit to live within us, the act of salvation continues to change our life to be more like Christ, and we begin to exhibit more Christ-like behavior as our spiritual conversion is manifested in our actions that follow. It is not the acts that bring about salvation, but salvation that brings about the acts.

Every sin that has ever been or will ever be committed by anyone has been paid for by Jesus when He died on the cross of Calvary. Three days and three nights following His burial, His bodily resurrection showed God's approval in what He had accomplished and confirmed there was nothing more required to satisfy sin's penalty.

Romans 1:3–4 Concerning his Son Jesus Christ our Lord, which was made of the seed of David according to the flesh; And declared to be the Son of God with power, according to the spirit of holiness, by the resurrection from the dead:

God now offers this redemption as a free gift to all who will call upon His name and accept it.

Romans 6:23 For the wages of sin is death; but the gift of God is eternal life through Jesus Christ our Lord.

Romans 10:13 For whosoever shall call upon the name of the Lord shall be saved.

WHAT MUST I BELIEVE TO BE SAVED?

You can buy bread without having to believe any of the science or chemistry involved in its production and you will get the same nutritional benefits as anyone else who buys the same bread and does believe. You can disbelieve the theory of gravity, but you are reminded it exists every time you throw something up toward the sky. There are many same-type examples where believing or not believing in something is not a requirement to get the same result. Salvation, on the other hand, requires that anyone considering becoming a Christian believe some fundamental truths before accepting Christ as his Savior.

First, you must confess you are a sinner. If you do not believe you are a sinner, then you will not see the need to get saved. The Bible tells us we are all sinners. If you are honest with yourself, you will come to the same conclusion.

Romans 3:10 As it is written, There is none righteous, no, not one:

Romans 3:23 For all have sinned, and come short of the glory of God;

Second, believe in God.

Hebrews 11:6 But without faith it is impossible to please him: for he that cometh to God must believe that he is, and that he is a rewarder of them that diligently seek him.

Our God is the Creator of the universe Who has made all things that exist. He is omnipotent (all-powerful), omniscient (all-knowing), and omnipresent (ever-present everywhere). Regarding His existence, He has always been and will always be—He simply just Is. When God commanded Moses to go to Egypt and lead the children of Israel out, Moses asked God how he would introduce Him to the people.

Exodus 3:13–14 And Moses said unto God, Behold, when I come unto the children of Israel, and shall say unto them, The God of your fathers hath sent me unto you; and they shall say to me, What is his name? what shall I say unto them? And God said unto Moses, I AM THAT I AM: and he said, Thus shalt thou say unto the children of Israel, I AM hath sent me unto you.

Third, you must believe that Jesus is the Son of God.

1 John 2:22–23 Who is a liar but he that denieth that Jesus is the Christ? He is antichrist, that denieth the Father and the Son. Whosoever denieth the Son, the same hath not the Father:

(but) he that acknowledgeth the Son hath the Father also.

1John 4:15 Whosoever shall confess that Jesus is the Son of God, God dwelleth in him, and he in God.

In the New Testament, Jesus made it very clear on many occasions that He is the Son of God, though many considered His claim blasphemous. This was one of the false charges the unbelieving Jews used against Him at His trial. Jesus was not just a prophet, a good teacher or philosopher, or just a good man with good intentions. He was God in human form with all His power and might yet willingly subjected to the frailties of a physical human body.

Philippians 2:5–8 Let this mind be in you, which was also in Christ Jesus: Who, being in the form of God, thought it not robbery to be equal with God: But made himself of no reputation, and took upon him the form of a servant, and was made in the likeness of men: And being found in fashion as a man, he humbled himself, and became obedient unto death, even the death of the cross.

Many have tried to downplay the genealogy of Jesus, trying to force him into a human mold with earthly parents, unwilling to believe He is the Son of God.

John 3:16–17 For God so loved the world, that he gave his only begotten Son, that whosoever believeth in him should not perish, but have everlasting life. For God sent not his Son into the world to condemn the world; but that the world through him might be saved.

Fourth, you must believe that Jesus died on the cross and was buried. On the evening after His crucifixion there were those who came to claim His body and give it a proper burial.

Mark 15:42–46 And now when the even was come, because it was the preparation, that is, the day before the sabbath, Joseph of Arimathaea, an honorable counselor, which also waited for the kingdom of God, came, and went in boldly unto Pilate, and craved the body of Jesus. And Pilate marveled if he were already dead: and calling unto him the centurion, he asked him whether he had been any while dead. And when he knew it of the centurion, he gave the body to Joseph. And he bought fine linen, and took him down, and wrapped him in the linen, and laid him in a sepulcher which was hewn out of a rock, and rolled a stone unto the door of the sepulcher.

It is plainly shown here that Pilate made sure that Jesus was dead on the cross before he allowed Joseph to take His body. Away with the claims that Jesus was removed from the cross while He was still alive and later recovered of His injuries!

Hebrews 9:15–17 And for this cause he is the mediator of the new testament, that by means of death, for the redemption of the transgressions that were under the first testament, they which are called might receive the promise of eternal inheritance. For where a testament is, there must also of necessity be the death of the testator. For a testament is of force after men are dead:

otherwise it is of no strength at all while the testator liveth.

These verses tell us that Jesus brought in a new testament, or will, and that any testament is only in effect after the death of the testator, or the one making the will. Thus, it was imperative that Jesus shed His blood and give His life to enforce His new will.

Fifth, you must believe that God raised Jesus from the dead.

Acts 13:29–30 And when they had fulfilled all that was written of him, they took him down from the tree, and laid him in a sepulcher. But God raised him from the dead:

This is the very cornerstone of the Christian faith. The death of Christ finished the work He had started on earth, as He had completed every task God gave Him. His death also completed the sin sacrifice that paved the way for anyone who calls upon Him to go to heaven.

1Corinthians 15:14 And if Christ be not risen, then is our preaching vain, and your faith is also vain.

As this verse suggests, if Christ did not rise from the dead, then our Christian service is wasted time, and we are believing in vain.

Christ's resurrection completed His ministry on earth, but just as important, His resurrection showed the power of God to defeat even death itself and revealed that He has the power to raise us from the dead as well. If Jesus had not risen, we would have reason to doubt His ability to raise us from the dead.

1Corinthians 15:17 And if Christ be not raised, your faith is vain; ye are yet in your sins.

If Jesus had not risen, then worse than not rising from the dead, we would still be guilty of all our sins and have no chance of heaven. But we know Jesus has risen. The tomb in Jerusalem is still empty just like the angel said on the morning of His resurrection.

Matthew 28:6 He is not here: for he is risen, as he said. Come, see the place where the Lord lay.

Sixth, you must believe that Jesus is the Savior.

John 8:24 I said therefore unto you, that ye shall die in your sins: for if ye believe not that I am he, ye shall die in your sins.

Jesus said these words to the unbelieving Jews that talked with Him. The Jews of that day looked for the coming Messiah, or Savior of the Jewish people prophesied in the Old Testament. Little did they understand, it was Jesus whom they sought, yet they did not grasp the concept. Their Savior stood in front of them and talked with them in person, but they did not recognize Him as such. They did not believe He was the One they had longed for. If we are going to pray to Jesus to be our Savior, we must certainly believe that He is the Savior.

John 6:29 Jesus answered and said unto them, This is the work of God, that ye believe on him whom he hath sent.

John 14:1 Let not your heart be troubled: ye believe in God, believe also in me.

Acts 4:12 Neither is there salvation in any other: for there is none other name under heaven given among men, whereby we must be saved.

1 John 2:22 Who is a liar but he that denieth that Jesus is the Christ? He is antichrist, that denieth the Father and the Son.

IS BELIEVING ENOUGH?

There are a lot of people that believe Jesus existed. Churches are full around the world every Sunday morning of those who profess that very fact. You probably know many of them or have seen them in your neighborhood. Some may go to church for every service, some only on Sunday morning, while others go only on special occasions like Easter and Christmas. Some of these people may believe all the things listed in the previous chapter and may, or may not, attend church on a regular basis. But is it enough to just believe an itemized list of facts to guarantee you a place in heaven? The Bible tells us that even Satan and his devils believe these things, yet they tremble at the reality of them, and they will not be in heaven.

James 2:19 Thou believest that there is one God; thou doest well: the devils also believe, and tremble.

Simply believing is not enough, no more than believing everything in the United States Constitution makes an Australian citizen an American citizen.

There are a lot of people resting their eternal destination on a simple belief system. They believe Jesus is the Son of God, that He has all the answers, and that He will take all true believers to heaven someday, which is all true, but they have done nothing with this information but believed it. Jesus said;

Matthew 7:21 Not every one that saith unto me, Lord, Lord, shall enter into the kingdom of heaven; but he that doeth the will of my Father which is in heaven.

How many people, today, are calling Jesus Lord and think they have a personal relationship with Him, but they have only believed a lot of facts and have never put their faith in Him or called upon His name to save them? You can believe a fire extinguisher will put out a fire, but if you never grab it and trust it to work when the flames start, you could lose everything. When it comes to your soul, the consequences of losing are incomprehensible.

Jesus said it plainly.

Johnn 3:3 Jesus answered and said unto him, Verily, verily, I say unto thee, Except a man be born again, he cannot see the kingdom of God.

You must be born again! As stated earlier, this is not a physical action, it is a spiritual transformation.

John 3:5 Jesus answered, Verily, verily, I say unto thee, Except a man be born of water and of the Spirit, he cannot enter into the kingdom of God.

Everyone has been born of water, which is a physical birth. But we must have the spiritual birth to enter heaven.

The spiritual birth occurs the moment a person accepts Jesus Christ as his Savior.

So, how does someone receive the spiritual birth? Unlike a special interest rate on a credit card, salvation is not something earned by being a good citizen, nor is it something we deserve for our good will. If we got what we deserved, we would all be in hell today. Likewise, learning is a big part of the Christian life, but we do not earn our salvation by accumulating credits in a classroom for religious study. Salvation is not a recipe, ritual, or confirmation that automatically enters your name on the role of heaven upon completion, though there is a logical process to arrive at the result.

Becoming a Christian is as easy as A, B, C. This idiom expresses how easy salvation is and offers abbreviations to help share it with others. The A is for admit. You must admit you are a sinner, which is the first item presented in the previous chapter of six things you must believe. No one that believes he is sinless will ever get saved. Why should they if there is nothing wrong with them? But the Bible tells us plainly that we have all sinned, so there is no escape from this indictment. We are all guilty.

Romans 3:10 As it is written, There is none righteous, no, not one:

Romans 3:23 For all have sinned, and come short of the glory of God;

Romans 5:12 Wherefore, as by one man sin entered into the world, and death by sin; and so death passed upon all men, for that all have sinned:

No one has the credentials to stand before God and enter heaven on their own, regardless of their personal achievements, material possessions, or political influence. God made us one and all, so how can we, the creature, achieve anything above our Creator?

Isaiah 55:8–9 For my thoughts are not your thoughts, neither are your ways my ways, saith the LORD. For as the heavens are higher than the earth, so are my ways higher than your ways, and my thoughts than your thoughts.

What is it that we can present to God in exchange for eternity in heaven? Everything we have has come from Him, and in a moment of time, He can take it all away.

James 1:17 Every good gift and every perfect gift is from above, and cometh down from the Father of lights, with whom is no variableness, neither shadow of turning.

We are but mere mortals incapable of providing anything on our own, much less the required blood sacrifice to pay for our individual sin, which is why Jesus had to pay the price for us.

Hebrews 2:9 But we see Jesus, who was made a little lower than the angels for the suffering of death, crowned with glory and honor; that he by the grace of God should taste death for every man.

1Peter 2:24 Who his own self bare our sins in his own body on the tree, that we, being dead to sins, should live unto righteousness: by whose stripes ye were healed.

We were born sinners, and we will die sinners, but we do not have to die without Jesus.

The letter B in our idiom stands for believe, which covers the remaining five items from the previous chapter. Remove any one of these five facts and everything changes. If God does not exist, then our concern for eternity is all in vain, life is all of chance, and we are left to our own devices till we die. If Jesus is not the Son of God, then He is the son of Joseph and has no claim to be an heir of God. If He was not dead when He was buried, then He was not raised from the dead but healed of an infirmity. If he was not resurrected, then God was not pleased with His life, or God's power is limited. If Jesus is not the Savior, then we have no hope.

If you have come this far, admitting you are a sinner and believing the facts about Jesus, and you have a desire to repent from your sin and turn your life over to God, then you are ready to exercise your faith and call upon the name of the Lord—letter C (call). This is a very personal decision that can only be made by you. No one can get saved for you, and you cannot get saved for anyone else. You do not pray to the sky, the ocean, the wind, or anything or anyone else. You pray to the God of creation Who made everything and everyone. It is His Son you are trusting for your eternity and placing your care in His hand. Your decision to accept Christ begins a very personal relationship with Him.

Romans 10:9–13 That if thou shalt confess with thy mouth the Lord Jesus, and shalt believe in thine heart that God hath raised him from the dead, thou shalt be saved. For with the heart man believeth unto righteousness; and with the mouth

*confession is made unto salvation. For the
Scripture saith, Whosoever believeth on him shall
not be ashamed. For there is no difference
between the Jew and the Greek: for the same Lord
over all is rich unto all that call upon him. For
whosoever shall call upon the name of the Lord
shall be saved.*

These verses teach us that our salvation starts with a
confession to God of the things we believe about Jesus. If
you are ready to make this profession of faith, and in a
place where you can do so, bow your head where you are
and close your eyes. This will show reverence to God and
help you to tune out what is going on around you.
Remember, this is not a ritual or recital of a specific
sequence of phrases, but a conversation from the heart
between you and the God of creation, our heavenly
Father. It is okay if you do not recite everything listed
verbatim, or that you verbally repeat everything listed.
After all, God already knows what you believe before you
ever start your prayer, but He wants to hear us confess it
to Him. What is important is that you mean what you say.
Yes, we can pray in silence from our heart and God will
hear it but dare to verbalize your prayer to let everyone
present know you truly believe. Call upon God to save
your soul and ask Him to place His Holy Spirit within you.

Becoming a Christian is not something yielded by
dispassionately following a mechanical formula or reciting
a specific sequence of words. Your prayer should be in
your own words and from the heart. Though many have
printed a Sinner's Prayer to repeat that has helped lead
many to Christ, I would rather offer the following
guidelines for you to use to formulate your own prayer.
The key is acknowledging your sinful state, your inability
to pay for your sin, your desire to be rescued from your

sin, and your total dependence on God to do something about it.

Begin your prayer by acknowledging God for who He is—the Almighty, Holy God of creation.

Confess to God what you believe about Jesus—He is the Son of God, He died for your sins, He was resurrected from the dead, and He is your Savior.

Express your desire to repent of, or turn from, your sin and turn to God.

By faith, ask God to save your soul from eternal damnation and invite the Holy Spirit into your life.

When you have finished your prayer, thank God for saving you. Live your life by faith, knowing God has made a difference.

HOW POWERFUL IS THE BLOOD OF CHRIST?

1Peter 1:18–19 Forasmuch as ye know that ye were not redeemed with corruptible things, as silver and gold, from your vain conversation received by tradition from your fathers; But with the precious blood of Christ, as of a lamb without blemish and without spot:

His blood is precious and incorruptible, above the value of any material possession we hold dear.

His blood purchased all believers (His Church).

Acts 20:28 Take heed therefore unto yourselves, and to all the flock, over the which the Holy Ghost hath made you overseers, to feed the church of God, which he hath purchased with his own blood

Ephesians 5:25–27 Husbands, love your wives, even as Christ also loved the church, and gave himself for it; That he might sanctify and cleanse

85

it with the washing of water by the word, That he might present it to himself a glorious church, not having spot, or wrinkle, or any such thing; but that it should be holy and without blemish.

Colossians 1:18 And he is the head of the body, the church: who is the beginning, the firstborn from the dead; that in all things he might have the preeminence.

Because of His blood, you will not face the wrath to come.

Romans 5:9 Much more then, being now justified by his blood, we shall be saved from wrath through him.

This does not mean that you will never have hardships or heartaches, as these are common in the sinful world we live in. This verse speaks of the wrath of God that is to be poured out on the world in the Day of Judgment mentioned in the book of Revelation, which Christians will not have to endure.

His blood has washed away our sins.

Colossians 1:12–14 Giving thanks unto the Father, which hath made us meet to be partakers of the inheritance of the saints in light: Who hath delivered us from the power of darkness, and hath translated us into the kingdom of his dear Son: In whom we have redemption through his blood, even the forgiveness of sins:

The blood of the sacrificial animals of the Old Testament only covered sin, thus it had to be continually repeated. The blood of Jesus paid the sin debt in full for the entire world, past, present, and future and made eternal salvation possible.

Hebrews 10:3–4 But in those sacrifices there is a remembrance again made of sins every year. For it is not possible that the blood of bulls and of goats should take away sins.

Hebrews 10:12 But this man, after he had offered one sacrifice for sins forever, sat down on the right hand of God;

1John 1:7 But if we walk in the light, as he is in the light, we have fellowship one with another, and the blood of Jesus Christ his Son cleanseth us from all sin.

Ephesians 1:7 In whom we have redemption through his blood, the forgiveness of sins, according to the riches of his grace;

Revelation 1:5 And from Jesus Christ, who is the faithful witness, and the first begotten of the dead, and the prince of the kings of the earth. Unto him that loved us, and washed us from our sins in his own blood,

His blood has enabled us to serve God. The annual atonement in the Old Testament covered the sins of Israel for another year and allowed God's blessings to go on uninterrupted. The animal sacrifices allowed the people to continue in God's favor and purified them to abide in His service. The blood of Christ is far superior to any of the Old Testament sacrifices. It does not just cover our sin; it removes it and purifies us for the works He calls us unto.

Hebrews 9:11–14 But Christ being come a high priest of good things to come, by a greater and more perfect tabernacle, not made with hands, that is to say, not of this building; Neither by the blood of goats and calves, but by his own blood he entered in once into the holy place, having obtained eternal redemption for us. For if the blood of bulls and of goats, and the ashes of a heifer sprinkling the unclean, sanctifieth to the purifying of the flesh: How much more shall the blood of Christ, who through the eternal Spirit offered himself without spot to God, purge your conscience from dead works to serve the living God?

His blood gives us access to the Father.

Hebrews 10:19 Having therefore, brethren, boldness to enter into the holiest by the blood of Jesus,

The Old Testament priests only went into the holiest part of the temple once a year to perform the sacrifice of atonement. The blood of Christ gives us unlimited access to God the Father at any time, day or night, and anywhere. We can talk to Him whenever we want about anything.

We see that Calvary has paid our sin debt and it will never require any additional sacrifice. The blood of Christ is sufficient for the sins of the entire world and its power reaches everywhere and is totally encompassing. For every believer, the blood of Christ has been applied to our life and saved us, and the Holy Spirit seals our salvation in this life to bring us into heaven.

We can see how all three, the Father, the Son, and the Holy Spirit work in our salvation. It is Christ Who gave Himself as the perfect sacrifice, God saves us when we repent, confess Christ, and call upon Him, and the Holy Spirit secures our salvation. Again, we see that our role is simply to acknowledge we are a sinner, repent from our sin, confess our belief in Jesus, and call upon God to save us. There are no works performed, no payments made; absolutely nothing on our part to earn our way to heaven!

Ephesians 2:8–9 For by grace are ye saved through faith; and that not of yourselves: it is the gift of God: Not of works, lest any man should boast.

I have never met anyone who was sorry they got saved, but if they did, too bad. There is nothing we can do to save us from our sin, and, thankfully, there is nothing we can do to cancel our salvation. The blood of Christ does not wear off like printing ink, and it does not go away like a rash. Nothing can get rid of it. But who would want to have their salvation denied? How would there ever come a time in a believer's life that they would regret their salvation experience and desire to go to hell?

John 10:27–29 My sheep hear my voice, and I know them, and they follow me: And I give unto them eternal life; and they shall never perish, neither shall any man pluck them out of my hand. My Father, which gave them me, is greater than all; and no man is able to pluck them out of my Father's hand.

John 6:37 All that the Father giveth me shall come to me; and him that cometh to me I will in no wise cast out.

1John 5:11–13 And this is the record, that God hath given to us eternal life, and this life is in his Son. He that hath the Son hath life: and he that hath not the Son of God hath not life. These things have I written unto you that believe on the name of the Son of God; that ye may know that ye have eternal life, and that ye may believe on the name of the Son of God.

1John 4:13–15 Hereby know we that we dwell in him, and he in us, because he hath given us of his Spirit. And we have seen and do testify that the Father sent the Son to be the Savior of the world. Whosoever shall confess that Jesus is the Son of God, God dwelleth in him, and he in God.

Is there anything that can erase our salvation? Absolutely nothing! Does this mean we can go do anything we want and still be saved? Absolutely! But be careful. Salvation is not a license to sin. The Bible tells us that there is a line we can cross with God, a sin unto death that can cut our life short.

Romans 6:16 Know ye not, that to whom ye yield yourselves servants to obey, his servants ye are to whom ye obey; whether of sin unto death, or of obedience unto righteousness?

We can allow our self to be a servant of sin for so long, and then God will bring us down.

Numbers 32:23 But if ye will not do so, behold, ye have sinned against the LORD: and be sure your sin will find you out.

Our liberty in Christ should not make us feel so comfortable and complacent that we are willing to continue in sin, knowing that God will not disown us. When someone who claims to be a Christian reaches this juncture in their life, they have a spiritual problem. If they are indeed a Christian, God will discipline them, just as our earthly father disciplined us as children.

Hebrews 12:6–8 For whom the Lord loveth he chasteneth, and scourgeth every son whom he receiveth. If ye endure chastening, God dealeth with you as with sons; for what son is he whom the father chasteneth not? But if ye be without chastisement, whereof all are partakers, then are ye bastards, and not sons.

If you find yourself involved in sin and God does not rebuke or convict you, it may be that you are not saved. Give yourself an honest appraisal. Have you truly repented from your sins? Do you recall a specific time when you confessed to God and asked Him to save you? No one can look into your heart and judge you for salvation, but other Christians can certainly look at your life to see if you are exhibiting Christ-like behavior, which is an acceptable form of judgment.

Maybe there are people (quite likely) that mistakenly think they are saved and have no conviction to stop sinning. They claim salvation because of a unique experience, a special feeling they had once, a set of events that mysteriously came together for them, or whatever. Maybe they plainly spoke a simple prayer and asked God to save them but never repented from their sin. This experience became a milestone for them that they blindly cling to for their eternal security, but it will only bring eternal disappointment if not dealt with in this life. These people will be like the ones Jesus spoke about, who do all the right things in this life but have never been truly converted.

Matthew 7:22–23 Many will say to me in that day, Lord, Lord, have we not prophesied in thy name and in thy name have cast out devils? and in thy name done many wonderful works? And then will I profess unto them, I never knew you: depart from me, ye that work iniquity.

WHAT IS THE BIBLE?

Composed of 66 books; 39 in the Old Testament, 27 in the New Testament

The Bible can be described as God's letter to mankind. In this letter, He presents creation, mankind's fall into sin, their attempt to gain favor with God on their own, their rejection of God in their lives, the gift of a Savior, the future of those who trust Christ as their Savior and those who reject him, and the final defeat of sin, death, and the grave.

Scoffers will tell you the Bible was written by a man, possibly many men, with their own agenda, but God declares Himself to be the author, though He used different men over many years to pen the words for us to read.

2 Peter 1:21 For the prophecy came not in old time by the will of man: but holy men of God spake as they were moved by the Holy Ghost.

God directed prophets in the Old Testament to write of His warnings to the Children of Israel, men to record events in Israel's history, Solomon to write the wealth of instruction from the book of Proverbs, and king David to write the comfort and encouragement of the Psalms.

In the New Testament, God led four men to record the events of the life of Christ while He was on earth, which we call the Gospels: Matthew, Mark, Luke, and John, with each book bearing their name. Luke was also used to record the history of the early Church in the book of Acts. Sequentially, the 21 books following the book of Acts were letters written to individuals or specific churches, 14 from the Apostle Paul. The last book of the Bible is the book of Revelation, which is a book of prophecy for future events yet to take place.

In its pages we learn how to live a life pleasing to God, to raise our family, to be a model citizen, to worship God, and to rejoice in His blessings. Its promises give us hope in times of trouble. Its truths give us a firm foundation on which to grow in our Christian lives.

The Bible is honest to tell us we are unworthy of any good thing, our best works are as filthy rags, and we are incapable of doing anything without God. It tells us we are sinners in need of a Savior.

Thankfully, it tells us of a Savior that died on the cross of Calvary, Who shed His blood to pay for our sin debt, and that by simple faith, we can trust Him to save our soul from hell.

The Bible can be intimidating. Because of its sheer size, at 783,137 words, many will never pick it up. Maybe they do not want to start reading it if they think they will not finish. But the Bible is not a novel that has to be read cover to cover for you to gain any benefit from it. There is something on every page of scripture for us to glean guidance for specific situations, direction for living our lives, or how-to instructions for learning to live peaceably with our fellow man. God wrote it for us, and He wants us to read it, believe it, obey it, memorize it, and share it.

Psalm 119:11 Thy word have I hid in mine heart, that I might not sin against thee.

Psalm 119:105 Thy word is a lamp unto my feet, and a light unto my path.

The wealth of knowledge contained in scripture can also be intimidating. I have heard men wax eloquently preaching on a Bible subject matter, demonstrating what must have taken hours of deep study to put together, and others who simply just scratched the surface of a particular topic. Is one better than the other? No! When presented properly, the Bible can be preached on any level and serve God's purpose. The same goes for our personal learning; we are not all Bible scholars. Some may think that they are expected to become a theologian if they ever start reading the Bible, so, instead of being embarrassed about not knowing everything about the Bible, they choose to learn nothing. Have you ever been asked, "Have you read your Bible today?" How would you answer? If you say, "Yes", the questioner may think you know more about the Bible than you really do. If you say, "No", others may question your desire to follow Christ. Be honest with yourself. Do not let your lack of biblical knowledge or intimidation from others hinder you from learning more. You are reading a book that was written by the God of heaven.

*Isaiah 55:11 So shall my word be that goeth forth
out of my mouth: it shall not return unto me void,
but it shall accomplish that which I please, and it
shall prosper in the thing whereto I sent it.*

The Bible is an exciting book. It tells of kings and
kingdoms, battles and victories, miracles, and prophecy.
There is no other text that will give you the true accounts
of creation, sin, the life of Christ, history of the Jewish
nation, and man's rescue from sin.

Remember that most all the events of the Bible took
place in a small geographical area, centered in the Middle
East. Though some of the names may be hard to
pronounce and unfamiliar to many of us, they are real.
Archaeologists continue to uncover ruins that offer
verification of people, places, and events mentioned in the
Bible, but these findings do not make the Bible true. The
Bible is true because God wrote it, and He says it is true.
Faith allows us to believe in the scriptures without
requiring archaeological verification.

*Psalm 119:160 Thy word is true from the
beginning: and every one of thy righteous
judgments endureth for ever.*

Many may think the Bible is antiquated, applicable only
to the days of old. "We are in a modern era," they say, "a
day of new ideas and innovation." But the Bible is just as
relevant today as it was the day the individual books were
penned.

Imagine the days of the ancient Roman emperors, the
Chinese dynasties, the Middle Ages, the Ottoman Empire,
the English monarchs, and the Industrial Revolution.
Today, we have our Technology Revolution, a time when

we believe man can do almost anything. The Bible has survived all these eras and, along the way, has been able to help and comfort all who have placed their trust in Christ. The Bible was not written to help man survive a period of time, which would have made it time dependent; rather, God has provided His Word to offer man eternal life, which is time independent. It is written for us, mankind, who were born in sin and have no way of escape except through the promises provided in the Bible.

WHAT IS FAITH?

We have used this word a lot throughout this book, but what does it mean? Is it important?

>*Hebrews 11:6 But without faith it is impossible to please him: for he that cometh to God must believe that he is, and that he is a rewarder of them that diligently seek him.*

Faith is important enough that without it we cannot please God, so we must demonstrate our faith. But what is faith?

Sometimes, the best commentary on the Bible is the Bible itself, where we can find the biblical definition of faith.

>*Hebrews 11:1 Now faith is the substance of things hoped for, the evidence of things not seen.*

In this verse, we see the word substance, which we typically take to mean an animate object or something we can hold in our hands. But this could also be a result, a resolution, or completion of a matter or event. For example, you may experience miraculous healing of a disease or impossible rescue from a hopeless situation. Neither of these examples brings about a physical object you can touch, but they each yield a recognized conclusion. The disease no longer has a hold on your body, or the hopeless situation is transformed to a pleasant outcome. For those brought through these situations, these results are their substances, or the things they had been hoping for.

The word hope connotes expressing a desire, not just to yourself, but to God, and believing that He can do something about it. We express these desires to God through prayer.

The second half of the verse tells us that the result was brought about by some means we cannot see or understand. For example, doctors sometimes cannot explain your physical recovery. Everything they tried seemed to fail or make the situation worse. But one day, without warning, they surprisingly see you healed. They examine you thoroughly but cannot find anything wrong. What happened to the disease that was ravaging your body? Why are your once failing organs suddenly working perfectly normal? Flabbergasted, they throw up their hands and can offer no explanation. They are beside themselves as they must admit your cure was nothing they had anything to do with. "It's a miracle," they may confess.

This is faith! You received the thing you were hoping for, and no one can offer a rational explanation for how it happened. There is no physical evidence to support the result. God has intervened on your behalf! You prayed and believed, and God heard and answered.

This example is extreme, but faith works on all levels.

The Bible is rife with people who exercised their faith in God. One great example is when Abraham left the land of his ancestry and went to a strange land God led him to. He did not know the country or anyone there, just that God said go, and he went. His hope, his prayer, was that God would take care of him, and time after time, God did. His faith in God was rewarded, as God gave all the land Abraham had trekked to his posterity.

What substance are you hoping for today? Is it a physical object like money, shelter, or food, or is it a change in circumstances or end of a conflict?

In the previous verse, Hebrews 11:6, the Bible says we must have faith to please God. How do we exercise faith to God? The verse tells us that "he that cometh to God must believe that he is." How do we come to God? We come through prayer. We bring Him our requests and desires, we express our love for Him, and we commune with Him as a friend. By praying to God, we are confessing that we believe He is; that is, we believe we are speaking with the One who made heaven and earth. We believe He exists, and we believe He hears our prayer. By faith, our prayer is not just words bouncing off the walls of the room we are in when we speak or residing only in our mind, but it is reaching the throne of God in heaven, and He is listening to us.

1 John 5:14 And this is the confidence that we have in him, that, if we ask any thing according to his will, he heareth us:

Do you sometimes think it strange that we serve a God we cannot see or prove His existence? Unbelievers find it bewildering. Some will argue there is no direct evidence of God or creation. I would suggest otherwise, but we cannot get into senseless debates with those whose minds will never be changed, regardless of what we have to say. The apostle Paul told Timothy;

1 Timothy 6:20 O Timothy, keep that which is committed to thy trust, avoiding profane and vain babblings, and oppositions of science falsely so called:

What we can do is present the gospel and let the Holy Spirit do His job to convict the listener's soul.

Romans 10:13–14 For whosoever shall call upon the name of the Lord shall be saved. How then shall they call on him in whom they have not believed? and how shall they believe in him of whom they have not heard? and how shall they hear without a preacher?

We cannot argue against the conviction of the Holy Spirit when we hear God's word preached or the tug on our heart the day we got saved. These are events that cannot be explained or rationalized. By faith, we believe it is God speaking to us. By faith, we believe He is the One making a difference in our lives.

Romans 8:16 The Spirit itself beareth witness with our spirit, that we are the children of God:

The next time someone asks you to prove God exists, you can tell them your job is to present the gospel, and God, through His Holy Spirit, will convince them of its authenticity.

THE PASTOR, THE PREACHER, THE MISSIONARY, AND THE EVANGELIST

These four terms are often used interchangeably, though each office is peculiar unto itself. I remember when I first became a Christian, I was unfamiliar with the true meaning of either. We all called our pastor, Preacher. I did not know what a missionary was, though our church supported several of them around the world. We had several evangelists visit our church, but I just labeled them all as preachers. Eventually, I learned the different distinctions, and I thought it would be a help to provide some clarification for a new Christian.

In the following verse, we see the offices God has established in the Church for edification.

Ephesians 4:11 And he gave some, apostles; and some, prophets; and some, evangelists; and some, pastors and teachers;

These are gifts bestowed on particular believers, each called by God, to fulfill their place of service in the Church. The apostles and prophets were necessary for guiding the early Church, and God used them to pen the books of the New Testament for the Church's instruction and doctrinal truths. These two offices no longer hold positions in the New Testament Church, as they were abolished with the completion of the scriptures.

1 Corinthians 13:9–10 For we know in part, and we prophesy in part. But when that which is perfect is come, then that which is in part shall be done away.

The New Testament is what has been perfected, or completed, and nothing is to be added to, or taken away from it. From Genesis to Revelation, Old Testament and New Testament, our Bible is finished. There are no additional future events to foretell (prophets) and no new doctrines from God to establish (apostles) outside of what is recorded in the Bible today.

This leaves us three groups from this verse: evangelists, pastors, and teachers.

The position of teacher is most self-explanatory. In reference to the Church, God calls men and women to present God's Word to those of all ages in a manner that promotes learning scripture. We grew up learning from teachers in secular schools, so we are quite familiar with their role. In the Church, it is very similar, in that people are separated by suitable age brackets and taught the Bible on a respective level.

Now let us look at the other two roles—pastor and evangelist—and see how preacher and missionary get connected.

Throughout the New Testament, Christians are likened unto sheep. As a whole, the Church makes up the flock, and Jesus proclaims Himself to be the Good Shepherd.

John 10:11 I am the good shepherd: the good shepherd giveth his life for the sheep.

In John 10:7–16, Jesus explains some of the things He does as our Sheperd. He looks out for our best interest, protects us, cares for us, knows us by name, and laid down His life for us. What more could you want from an overseer?

The word pastor means shepherd. In the local church, the pastor is the shepherd of the congregants, or the sheep. Since Jesus is the Good Shepherd, the pastor is referred to as the under-shepherd, as his position is to lead the church as Christ leads him.

His job, too, is to protect the flock he has been entrusted with, to pray for them, to be concerned for them, to preach to them, to teach them, and to equip them the best he can to serve the Lord. With this, it is our responsibility as believers to love our pastor, follow his leadership, to seek God's guidance in our lives, and to serve the Lord. We are to serve the Lord together.

Note that one of the responsibilities of the pastor is to preach, or to proclaim, the Bible to the church. This may be a very simple proclamation, or sermon, on a particular event in scripture, or it could be a very deep sermon regarding a specific church doctrine. In all of these instances, the pastor is God's messenger conveying to the congregation the message for the hour. Every believer also has the responsibility to proclaim the scriptures to those we meet, so we are technically preaching to others also, but only those called of God to lead a congregation can be a pastor.

Never think it is the pastor's responsibility to do all the work of the church while the congregants sit idle. It is every believer's responsibility to take the gospel to a lost and dying world. The Great Commission (Matthew 28:19–20) was commanded of all believers.

Matthew 28:19–20 Go ye therefore, and teach all nations, baptizing them in the name of the Father, and of the Son, and of the Holy Ghost: Teaching them to observe all things whatsoever I have commanded you: and, lo, I am with you alway, even unto the end of the world. Amen.

Verse 19 says go! Go where? To all nations! The Church is to go to all the nations of the world to preach and teach the gospel of Jesus Christ and to win as many as possible to the kingdom of God. Does this mean we all must travel around the world? Certainly not. Not everyone can go. But there are some that God separates for this task, and we call them missionaries. The rest of us will stay behind and pray and support them as they go in our place.

The word missionary is not in the Bible, but we have several examples to follow of what other men have done to evangelize people groups beyond their locale. The first missionaries, or sent ones, introduced to us in scripture are Barnabas and Saul (later named Paul).

Acts 13:1–3 Now there were in the church that was at Antioch certain prophets and teachers; as Barnabas, and Simeon that was called Niger, and Lucius of Cyrene, and Manaen, which had been brought up with Herod the tetrarch, and Saul. As they ministered to the Lord, and fasted, the Holy Ghost said, Separate me Barnabas and Saul for the work whereunto I have called them. And when they had fasted and prayed, and laid their hands on them, they sent them away.

Barnabas and Saul were called of God to go to a specific location and preach the gospel. When God's call was revealed to the Church, the Church fasted and prayed for them and sent them away to their task. The men obeyed God's call, and many souls were saved and churches established in the areas they traveled.

Today, God still calls men to the mission field. Those who answer the call, willfully give themselves to His desire and follow His leading to wherever it may take them. For those who are not called to go, our responsibility is to pray for the missionary and his family and to financially support them to get the job done there, while we get the job done in our community.

There are Christians whom God has endowed the special give of evangelism. That is, they have the gift of presenting scripture in an enlightening way that the Holy Spirit uses to convict the hearts that hear it and bring them to the saving knowledge of Jesus Christ. This is the evangelist.

The evangelists I have witnessed have an encouraging disposition, an infectious smile, and energy to preach the gospel. Their presentation is usually spot-on, right to the heart of the listener. The most convicting messages I have heard have come from evangelists.

Like the missionary, the evangelist has a church home, but he spends most of his time away, traveling to other churches, special meetings, conferences, and other events where he is invited to preach and/or hold revival meetings. The evangelists I know travel all over the United States and occasionally abroad, anywhere for someone to hear the gospel.

In summary, we see the pastor is the one called by God to lead a local assembly. His responsibilities are great as the under-shepherd. We need to pray for our pastor and his family and encourage him.

The preacher can be anyone who proclaims the truth of God's Word to someone else. We usually think of this as the pastor delivering a message from the pulpit, which is an important responsibility for the pastor. Though every pastor can preach, not every preacher can pastor. I can preach, or be a witness, to my friends, but I am not called to be a pastor.

The missionary is called by God to take the gospel to a specific region or country. This usually means taking his wife and kids well beyond their family and friends. It is a sacrifice they are willing to make for souls to be saved.

The evangelist is called by God to travel as directed, and to present the gospel in a way that convicts of sin and brings the lost to Christ and the saved closer to Christ.

FINAL THOUGHTS

As a new Christian, it is imperative you strive to live your life for God. Find a good Baptist Church to join, a church that preaches the gospel, uses the King James Bible, supports worldwide evangelism, sings God-honoring music, and provides ministries you can serve in. Through consistent church attendance and personal Bible study, you will grow in wisdom, be strengthened by other Christians, honor God with your service, and learn to reach others with the gospel. You will also see God change your perspective, desires, ambition, and possibly your vocation as you strive to become more like Christ. You may not know what God has in store for you yet, but He does have a plan for your life, let Him work it.

Colossians 3:17 And whatsoever ye do in word or deed, do all in the name of the Lord Jesus, giving thanks to God and the Father by him.

Colossians 3:23 And whatsoever ye do, do it heartily, as to the Lord, and not unto men;

Develop a consistent prayer life. Remember, we are sinners saved by grace, and as sinners, we will sin. We need to ask God to forgive us of our sins every day, not to keep us saved, as that has been settled, but to keep us spiritually clean so God will hear our prayers and continue to use us.

Psalm 66:18 If I regard iniquity in my heart, the Lord will not hear me:

You belong to God, now and He wants to use you for His specific purpose. Jesus has paid the price for your sin and saved you from eternity in hell.

1 Corinthians 6:20 For ye are bought with a price: therefore glorify God in your body, and in your spirit, which are God's.

Be a faithful witness to others around you. Let them see the change in your life. Do not hide the gospel from anyone.

2 Corinthians 4:3 But if our gospel be hid, it is hid to them that are lost:

Romans 1:16 For I am not ashamed of the gospel of Christ: for it is the power of God unto salvation to every one that believeth; to the Jew first, and also to the Greek.

Guard your heart and mind to be pure.

Philippians 4:8 Finally, brethren, whatsoever things are true, whatsoever things are honest, whatsoever things are just, whatsoever things are pure, whatsoever things are lovely, whatsoever things are of good report; if there be any virtue, and if there be any praise, think on these things.

2 Thessalonians 3:3 But the Lord is faithful, who shall stablish you, and keep you from evil.

Be encouraged that God will empower you to do whatever He calls you to do.

Philippians 4:13 I can do all things through Christ which strengtheneth me.

ABOUT THE AUTHOR

Keith Brumbalow has been a Sunday school teacher for over 35 years, in the same church he was saved at in 1980, where he is still a member. He currently resides in Texas with his wife of over 45 years. His desire is to write books to help others and hopefully to write a novel someday.

www.ingramcontent.com/pod-product-compliance
Lightning Source LLC
Chambersburg PA
CBHW061750020426
42331CB00006B/1420